# PSYCHOLOGICAL DYNAMICS
# IN RELIGIOUS LIVING

# PSYCHOLOGICAL DYNAMICS IN RELIGIOUS LIVING

CHARLES A. CURRAN

Herder and Herder

1971
HERDER AND HERDER NEW YORK
232 Madison Avenue, New York 10016


Nihil obstat: Leo J. Steady, Censor Librorum
Imprimatur: ✠ Robert F. Joyce, Bishop of Burlington
August 11, 1971


Library of Congress Catalog Card Number: 72-170968
© 1971 by Herder and Herder, Inc.
Manufactured in the United States

# Contents

# Acknowledgments

FOR the collaboration that aided in the production of this book, special recognition should go to Daniel D. Tranel and Jennybelle P. Rardin.

Particular appreciation is due Rosina M. Gallagher.

In addition, a special debt is owed students and associates at Loyola University as well as Roland Janisse and Norma Gutierrez and members of institutes at the University of Windsor and elsewhere and, in particular, the Benedictine Sisters of Chicago, for understanding, discussion and helpful clarifications, when many of these ideas were first presented to them.

Charles A. Curran

*He who does not love, remains in death.*

*I John 3:14*

# Introduction

IT is a commonplace today to speak of man as alienated and estranged from himself and from those around him. This has been amply documented by such writers as David Riesman, Herbert Marcuse, Marshall McLuhan, and many others. It is, moreover, the recurrent theme of nearly all existentialist writing. Various explanations have been brought forth to explain this condition of modern man, ranging from the impact of technology to an inherent anxiety that is the birthright of us all. To the extent that these writers have brought attention to man's plight and have suggested remedies for it, they have performed a real service.

The attempts on the part of people to cope with their sense of discomfort and alienation in the face of the unknown have run the gamut from T-Groups to Hippie Communes. All these people have one thing in common and that is the desire to achieve a sense of belonging, of worth, and of meaning. In view of this, the definition of man as a "religious animal" takes on greater significance. Whatever man does, even his most abject failures, represents his struggle to create a bond with something beyond himself. This would be the literal meaning of the word "religion." It is only in achieving such a bond that he can extricate himself from his alienation.

This book aims to set forth the basic conditions that

9

would seem necessary for man to redeem himself in some measure from his alienated state. Yet it would be misleading for one to think that by merely being aware of these conditions he will automatically arrive at that goal of happiness and fulfillment that we all seek. In that sense, therefore, what is said in this book is not necessarily new. The basic means for man to achieve that unity which he desires have always been present, granting that at times they may have been obscured throughout the course of history. What is new, however, is the way in which these means have application to our own time.

We might think of man not only as a "religious animal," but as a "community animal." We immediately see the word "unity" in "community," and man seeks unity in all that he does. We will begin, therefore, with a discussion of the nature of genuine community and what is necessary for it to be brought about. This will lead, in Chapter II on "Celibacy as Authentic Communication," to a consideration of one's state in life as either enhancing or defeating genuine communication. In Chapters III and IV, we will speak of the Church, regarded as "persons," as the ideal community, ultimately described as "The Redemptive Community."

We will have seen that basic to any communication is not only a communicator but also a listener. This theme will be developed in Chapter V. Assuming that one actually achieves unity and communication with himself and others, he is still lacking in ultimate fulfillment. He, therefore, must communicate beyond himself and others to the Total Other, and this he does through prayer. Consequently, we speak in Chapter VI of "The Dynamics of Prayer." Not only must man listen in order for communication to take place and trust in prayer, however; he must also be able to believe. Therefore, we will address ourselves, in Chapter VII to the question, "What Can Man Believe In?"

In Chapter VIII we come about full circle. Before man can be in community and communion with another, and finally with the Total Other, he must be in communion with himself. He does this by Being a Friend to Himself.

# I. The Creative Community

THE issue that we are initially concerned with is that of genuine communication. In considering this issue, the relationship between men and women might serve as a model. Such a model would contain the same richness for men-to-men and women-to-women communications. One can add new freshness to the question of masculine-feminine relationships by considering a traditional notion that occurs in the Classics, and is also suggested in the writings of St. Paul. This is the notion of the androgen.

## ANDROGEN MODALITY

In ancient Greek philosophy, the ideal state of the human personality is the androgen, from the Greek *andros* (aner), meaning man, and *gyne*, meaning woman. This suggests an element of incompletion about the human personality, not merely from the physiological side, but more importantly, from a psychological viewpoint. The resultant interpretation that the man completes the woman and the woman completes the man, thus making the man the head and the woman the heart, is somewhat inadequate, however. Although for a long time it has been viewed that way, and women have continually fit into that pattern, nevertheless there seems to be less and less justification for it.

What is more basically at issue is the need that each person has to complete himself through the sex in which

13

he is not clearly defined. In order to fulfill this need, the person must go out of himself in and through the opposite undefined sexual phase of himself. Thus, for example, a man would go out of his masculinity through the feminine side of himself to the woman. He cannot really reach a woman except to the extent that he feminizes himself; and in like manner, when a woman attempts to go out to a man, what she must do is to masculinize herself in some measure.

A linguistic model can be of help in seeing this more clearly. Of all the international marriages, the most common ones were those of the American G.I.'s. In those marriages, it was most often the woman, married to the American, who came back to America speaking English; the reverse was seldom true where the American husband learned to speak the language of his wife. In this linguistic model one of the first weaknesses of our culture and therefore of many of the phases of men-women relationships becomes apparent. This weakness is that the culture has determined a structure wherein it is primarily the woman's responsibility to develop her 'M' in order to relate to the man. This produces a lack of perspective and sensitivity to her on the part of the man. There is little expectation of the man developing his 'F' in order to relate to the woman. As a result, the man does not "step out" to femininity, and he thus deprives the woman, and the total relationship, of its potential richness.

In exploring the subtleties of genuine communication, two difficulties can be confronted: one centers around men relating to men and women relating to women; and the other is the guilt, such as the guilt of homosexuality under the guise of "particular friendship," that arises out of men-to-men and women-to-women relationships. This kind of guilt results from a failure to develop the androgen modality. By proposing an androgen modality of com-

14

munication, both men and women can be freed from the anxiety and guilt around homosexuality, since it seems obvious that two women can be genuine friends, or two men can be genuine friends. One might even say that there could be a genuine friendship, in a true androgenic sense, in one woman at times masculinizing the other and vice versa. This would involve, however, on the part of both persons, sufficient security in their own sexuality to allow each to be masculine or feminine as the communication creatively progressed. In this communication, the "F" would be the understanding *logos* and the "M" would be the generating need.

## THE UNDERSTANDING LOGOS

The notion of the understanding *Logos* is in the Augustinian tradition of the Trinity. The understanding *logos* could be considered feminine as well as masculine, the generating principle is masculine, and the creative relationship between them is love, or the Holy Spirit. In such a communication there is no question about whether the relationship is between two men or two women or a man and a woman. While the *logos* is "F" in the Trinitarian community, it becomes the redemptive "M" that penetrates the world, as Christ came into the world. Out of this is generated a response which, if it is to be creative, requires that the other—the world—change from "M" to "F." Otherwise there will be two "M's" battling one another for power rather than engagement in a mutual fulfillment.

## "M" AND "F" IN COMMUNITY

This "M-F" image might be applied to God, since one might say that the *genitus* in God relates to a logos, but in a divine sense. Herein one sees the great abstractive power of Augustine, for he was talking about human relation-

15

ships. What he perceived was that if the "M" and "F" interaction is so profoundly a redemptive and godly act, then one person's creative life-impulse can totally reflect another person. This reflection, therefore, would be the most godly kind of human communication. It is divinizing and, as such, it is the opposite of diabolism. It is the very best relationship that exists between men, where one's *logos* (understanding) and the other's *genitus* (penetration) creates the deepest kind of love between them. This is profoundly creative, effulgent, and diffusive of itself, because it is constantly pouring itself out.

If this pouring out constitutes the creative community, then what Augustine has been saying is that it represents the best that we have as a reflection of God. The core of the doctrine of the Trinity is that God is a perfect community. Opposite to every projection of the *genitus* there is an equally responsive *logos*, or understanding. St. John begins with the Platonic *logos*: "In the beginning was the Word, and the Word was with God and the Word was God." Then, "The Word became flesh," that is, "F" became "M," "and dwelt among us." But we, because of our death-impulse, did not know Him. But those who overcame their death-impulse and did know Him are the children of life and light. God is the perfect androgen. St. Paul says there is neither Jew nor Gentile, neither male nor female, neither Greek nor pagan. What a creative relationship brings about, therefore, is greater integration and less segmentation.

The ideal community would be a sensitive, "perceptual feel," so that when one person starts to speak, the whole response will be "F." Because of the open "F" receptivity, the death-impulse, or the effects of Satan,* in an older

*Throughout this treatment we are speaking of "satanism" psychologically, not theologically.

16

terminology, has not gotten hold of the communicator. This means that a creative relationship is made possible by the initial receptivity and openness of the hearers which, in turn, allows the communicator to make an "F" response back to them in each of their "F" needs. Such would be the experience of community filled with grace, with gracefulness or gracility, in contrast to a damning death-experience. For Augustine it was the breathing forth of a "Spirit" or "sigh" of love, between two persons in an intense communion, which provides the model for understanding another. The other then trustfully gives himself without fear, restraint, or anxiety. This is the Christian solution to the alienation that besets society today, as well as in former times.

## THE "F": EVE OR MARY

To be noted about Eve, in the Garden of Eden narrative, is that she has maximum power because *andro* alone is incomplete. There must be another to take *andro,* Adam, from alienation. This other is both like Adam and different. The difference is the "F" element, the responsive, receptive element, not only in the physiological connotation of the sexual act, but in the "F" symbolization. The power of "F" lies in Adam's being alienated and alone, and it is "not good for him to be alone." He needs Eve. He needs the receptive, understanding person to whom he can communicate his life principle. When a person generates, that is, when he goes out to another, he needs a corresponding *logos,* as we indicated earlier, to understand, to reflect, to respond. This will then produce love in imitation of the Third Person, the intense bond of love, the Holy Spirit.

Eve, then, had power over Adam by virtue of her "F" which was to be used in a creative relationship to complete

17

them both. But instead of exercising her "F," she was defeated by her own death-instinct. Understood literally, the snake overcame Eve and she overcame Adam. When Adam's life-principle came forward as a communication with her, contrary to all the other times when she was redemptive and fulfilling, on this occasion she destroyed it. Consequently, evil came into the world. Eve's death-instinct overcame her life-urge and Adam was defeated. The only alternative was to move out from that great place of joy, communion, and sharing.

The nature of the sin here would be that while one person wants to have incarnate understanding and redemption, the other person fails to give it. This failure or refusal to give understanding satisfies the will to power. If Adam is alienated and alone, then each time that he opens himself up to Eve, he conveys maximum power on her either to demean or to convalidate him.

The nature of the self-defeating mechanism is also evident here. Having demeaned Adam, Eve too must leave the Garden; thus, she has demeaned herself as well. But her own demeaning came only after that of Adam. Her death-impulse, responding to his life-impulse, has affected them both. Therefore, grace, internalized, would mean that one's life-forces would overcome the death forces of the other. Instead of reverting to alienation and defeat, one would continually struggle to overcome the death-forces in the other. This would allow the other eventually to respond to his own life-forces. Love is seen when one's life-urge is victorious over the death-urges of another, and in the ensuing open and trusting relationship they have a convalidating, creative communication. Instead of defeat, bitterness, and death, there is a flaming, living, creative exaltation, a resurrection together.

The resurrection together alludes to the figures of

both Christ and Mary. The "F" in Mary in contrast to Eve, represents the life-impulse. When one "F" comes forward in victorious, convalidating redemption, there results the life of love, a life of gratitude and fruition.

## THEO-PSYCHOLOGY

Perhaps a good way to consider a death-wish relationship would be through theo-psychology. Leaving theology in its own order, and looking at man clinically, one sees in him an open-endedness that seems to demand the aspect of "theo." Man is not an anthropocentric individual; he is actually theocentric, whether he is an atheist or not. In his "project to become God," as Sartre calls it, none of his activities provides him with total fulfillment. If the person is a believing theist, then he sees that only God can fulfill him; if he is an atheist, then there seems nothing for him but final frustration or, to state it another way, he becomes a frustrated god. Thus, no matter how one views man, the "theo" aspect of him must be considered.

From the point of view of theo-psychology, then, it can be suggested that the primitive or primary tendency in the adult or in the child is to blame the other, to put evil "out there." This represents an attempt to hold on to one's deification. It is always someone else who failed, who did something wrong, not the person himself; it is an evil creature "out there" who is behind all evil. Satan is thus the reverse side of a redemptive figure because if Satan is the cause of evil, then the individual need not be blamed because he himself is not really evil. It is just that he has "devils" in him.

When it is used in this sense, what the satanic element describes, is an outward projection of a person's guilt or anxiety that he cannot effectively cope with. When someone comes forth with a life-urge or a life-statement, his

19

normal expectancy is to have that life-urge positively reinforced so that he would be redeemed and convalidated in it. He could then leave the other's presence feeling more creative and more fulfilled than he was before.

What happens, however, is that the satanic element, or death-urge, enters in and the opposite occurs. Having taken the risk to reveal one's enthusiasm and openness and sincerity of feeling, the other diabolically destroys him. Internalized, this would be seen as the powers of darkness against the powers of light, or the powers of death against the powers of life. St. Paul presents this notion in the tradition of diabolism, where the satanic or death forces are "out there"; but internalized, it is Freud's idea that matching every strength one has for life, there is an almost equal strength for death. Psychological diabolism is one's life-wish embattled with a powerful force that is his death-wish. Satanic elements, in one sense, would be one's projection of his death-wish outward. The devil is among us because we cannot handle our own death-wish. One could see this aspect of diabolism as a possible theo-psychological explanation of the disillusionment of the human encounter. Contrary to one's expectations that another will redeem him, he ends up being condemned, or being made to look foolish. The idea of Satanism as internalized as the death-wish, will be explored in greater detail in Chapter V, on "The Need for Creative Listeners."

A consideration of one's general dissatisfaction with himself leads to something that is both obvious and not obvious at the same time. This is the contention that each person has the project to become God, as suggested by Sartre, and to which we alluded previously. It is the first and most violent vector of one's frustration. If man's project is to become God, then all other people should be quasi-divine or else he will be bitter and frustrated towards them. They will all disappoint him because he will always be disappointing to himself since he is not, in fact, God.

In this situation, one will be bitter towards himself. But his bitterness towards himself is so painful that he must disguise it in the form of being bitter towards others. Man is not merely a rational animal, but he is also a rationalizing animal, and very often he rationalizes before he becomes rational. His first way of dealing with a situation is to blame the other and then to use all his powers of rationalization to justify what is wrong with the other. This protects him because he remains an unexamined divinity; the "trouble" lies with other people. Human beings have disappointed him but he himself can still remain "God."

If one examines the way in which that kind of protective person speaks, there is, in fact, a god-quality about it. By blaming other people or other organizations, he can hold himself in a state of divinity which will justify his condemnation of others. But there is no incarnation here and no redemption. The way one maintains his state of divinity is to attack "out there" and never look at himself.

The cynic, for example, is preserving his own divinity because he refuses to enter into humanity. He is an inhuman, non-incarnate, non-redemptive judge. He is a cruel judge because he recognizes no human weakness, not being human himself. For him, others must function in a divinized way, since he himself is divine. The way to demean, to embitter, and to spread destruction in a group is to set oneself up as divinized and as above all human limitations.

The one impulse, then, that always frustrates man and makes him the victim of self-attack is his project to

21

become God. Man is a creature in constant rebellion against being a creature; he wants, at least, to be an angel, a purely abstractive being who sees things always with intellectual clarity. He does not want to be asked to do anything in the incarnate world. That is for others to do, and while they are doing it, he will criticize them and continually point out how inadequate they are.

David E. Lilienthal, after many years of organizational experience, wrote:

The short and sure road to despair and surrender is this: to believe that there is, somewhere, a scheme of things that will eliminate conflict, struggle, stupidity, cupidity, personal jealousy. The idea of Utopia is mischievous, as well as unrealistic. And dull, to boot. Man is born pushing and shoving as the sparks fly upward.*

## BALANCED COMMUNITY RELATIONSHIP

Authorities in religious living have always warned against "trying too hard." The tradition of religious life has tried to maintain a balance in striving for anything connected with divinity. The danger has been that of catapulting oneself from the grandeur of a mystical pursuit to the misery of trying to derive from physical impulses and sensations all the intensity of reality that one's divinized urges are seeking. This is so even in the case of mysticism, or any religious impulse that does not have the right kind of cylindering and the right kind of containment. It is the classical "corruption of the best is the worst." In trying so hard for some kind of authentic relationship in a religious growth towards achieving the God-project, there is the danger at any point of total failure.

The result of such failure is a tragic frustration in the opposite direction. Having bounced from the extreme of

*David E. Lilienthal, *The Journals of David E. Lilienthal: The Harvest Years*, 1959–1963, New York, 1971.

22

an inauthentic mysticism to the extreme of sensory satisfaction, one is suddenly and tragically aware of his limitations. For example, a person can enjoy for only a very
limited time the taste of food, music in his ear, sensation
in his hands, or some kind of sexual fulfillment. But
a life-time of this kind of pursuit is so extremely limited
that with one taste of sense fulfillment, a person experiences the incarnate reality of the moment, and then
is soon satiated and once again he is caught up in his
divinized bitterness. Alcoholism, drug-addiction or even
overeating or any of the primitive needs that can victimize
a person in the physiological order, might represent
an attempt to give some surcease to these compensatory
impulses.

But any purely physical experience, sought as a relief
and an escape, results in an ultimate let-down because the
physical need is quickly saturated and satiated; no human
condition, no human relationship, no human person can
fulfill a man's divinized need. One can then be left with
blaming others. They are wrong, they disillusion him, they
embitter him, they do things to him. If a community
relationship is to have any balance, an internalization of
the need to face oneself will be necessary. Otherwise one
is rebounding between some kind of physical fulfillment of
a temporary nature, and projecting bitterness on to others
when this is saturated.

## FRUITION IN THE COMMUNITY

Filled with the magnificence of what they are for each
other, the members of a community exercise what St.
Peter calls a "royal priesthood" in the pursuit of their own
excellence. In this way the Christian ideal comes out to be
horizontal rather than vertical. In the creative convalidation of one another, all the excellences of the two people,

23

or of the group, are mounted to the maximum of each one's unique potentiality.

If this could happen in St. Peter's time, if the early Christians could bring this about, and if, in moments of deep psychological awareness, T-groups, sensitivity groups, learning groups, and counseling groups can produce the same thing, then this seems to be the future of the community. Whether the relationship is one of women to women, men to men, or men to women, the issue centers around an "M" and an "F" communication. We can see now more clearly how the model would be the androgen, which is neither "M" nor "F."

Thus people are "sacraments" to one another, and each can be made holy only through the other. This is a movement away from things "out there," to the inner life-forces that make one holy. Every creative relationship between people is as a new child. While everyone is dedicated to propagation, this is the kind of propagation that is inherent in the priesthood and that gives meaning to celibacy.

Aquinas makes the point that insofar as one chooses not to propagate physically it can only be for the greater benefit of the human race. While one can indeed benefit the human race by physically propagating, there are other ways in which he can benefit the human race even more. It is this that would justify his not propagating physically. Unless, then, as we will discuss later, the life of the priest, the nun, or of any celibate person shows greater evidence of commitment to the community than the lives of married people, they are indeed bachelors and old maids. They are the "cursed" people of the human race in the biblical tradition of sterility. For if their lives are no more than that of bachelors and old maids, they are fraudulent.

Considered from this point of view, each person who

does not propagate physically has a great responsibility to the community. The responsibility is even greater for the professional person whose children would be among the bright and achieving. They are in a grave position if they deny those children to the human race. This would be the reasoning of Aquinas: whatever one does, he must do it far beyond himself for the sake of the human race. Such is the meaning of being commanded to propagate. It actually means that we are commanded to be creative in and through each other. Only in this way is propagation also love.

The basis of this creative relationship, therefore, which is the heart of community, is the convalidating of each person in the relationship. The key word is "convalidating." Each person sees his own unique value in the way that others relate to him. His "M" or "F" is enhanced, his needs are fulfilled, his creative drives are encouraged, and he himself is not absorbed in the process. If one were to be devoured, the relationship would be a purely narcissistic one. To be truly creative, the relationship must be such that it brings about the positive aspects for each person, so that each does not simply leave drained of and by the other; rather, each is encouraged in the direction of his own personal quest. Each person's life would be enhanced and his sense of self-esteem *convalidated*. The "con" refers to the relationship between the two, and the "validation" means that they are equally validated, equally redeemed, equally of greater self-worth as they see themselves reflected in the other. The obvious opposite of this would be destructive and non-convalidating, where one's relationship with another would leave him less sure of himself, discouraged, less able to go ahead with whatever project he is working on, and more urged to withdraw

25

## INCARNATE EXCELLENCE

The struggle involved in a creative relationship is for incarnate excellence. But where does this exist? How is it brought about between people? Since most Americans are immigrants, for example, or from an immigrant culture, they do not have the ability to bring out each one's own excellence in a way that the *noblesse oblige* in another culture would be able to do. In an upper-class tradition, the *noblesse oblige* could be depended upon to receive excellence from one another and from their homes. The schools did not have to confer it upon them.

But modern man is victimized by a lack of self-worth. His culture has not provided it for him, and so he must depend upon the existential moment for convalidation from his fellow man. This is because he has almost nothing from his tradition. Therefore, he needs to be convalidated here and now. This is the incarnate excellence that democracy proposes. It proposes an excellence, not in a nobility that is "obliged," but an excellence that is in everyone with a corresponding obligation to one another. This is what might be called a democratic incarnate excellence.*

The possibility of interpreting this excellence as equality, however, was precisely the great fear directed against democracy. Among the ancient Greeks, the "demos" was a very negative concept because of their fear of the demeaning quality or littleness in the value system of the "masses." Perhaps the notion of appointment from above, assuming it were not fraudulent and that it had a certain genuine nobility about it, might sometimes be

*This question and that of leadership is discussed in detail in *Religious Values in Counseling and Psychotherapy*, New York: Sheed and Ward, 1969, pp. 327–352.

better. It was not necessarily always bad or tyrannical. What democratic structures raise as a special issue is how to devise adequate means to find and promote genuine leadership from its own group. Without this, it will demean itself in its leaders

## THE MAGNANIMOUS MAN

Whether in a democratic or aristocratic structure, however, the leader demonstrates his personal nobility by a special kind of courage and self-giving that is magnanimous. In developing this point at greater length, Aquinas gives the magnanimous courage of an added dimension by tying up, to some degree, leadership and celibacy. Celibacy would be the mean between "loutishness" and "old-maidishness" on the one hand, and sexual intemperance on the other. Men avoiding women and women avoiding men, rather than simply avoiding the venereal relationship, would be, in this sense, both withdrawal and intemperance.

Aristotle and Aquinas distinguish between two kinds of people: those who are normally courageous—the ordinary person, the mass of the people; then there is the person who goes beyond ordinary courage, and he is magnanimous. This latter is the man who has broad vision and who, in popular psychological terminology, would be the leader. If one were looking for leaders, he would look for the magnanimous, and if he were testing for leadership, he would look for two different reactions. Courageous people would react in a limited way, but magnanimous people would react in the extreme. But they do not violate the mean by reacting in the extreme because their reasons for doing so are balanced.

From this point of view, the magnanimous are reacting on a higher plane, which simply means not superiority but that on "the mountain" they can see much farther ahead than can the people on the lower level. Therefore, their planning has greater breadth to it even though those on the lower level do not see the point of it here and now.

The magnanimous man, then, does what is most becoming to his broader vision. He is true to himself. But what is becoming for him can be, in fact, an extreme project for the ordinary man. Magnanimity means "bigness of soul" which would be the inner psychological attitude or inner psychological world. This is matched by another virtue which Aquinas calls magnificence. In the word "magnificence," the emphasis is on *facere*. Obviously the magnanimous man must also be magnificent, in the sense that from his inner magnanimity he goes out to magnificent projects. Therefore he *does* things with a breadth of vision that is startling to others who are "little-minded." Aquinas does not intend this as a pejorative term; rather, others are narrow-visioned, or small-minded, so they are "small-project" people.

## CONVALIDATING RESPONSE

Aquinas's point is that the magnanimous man is audacious but not fool-hardy. For example, many projects fail because people are too little-minded to spend enough money on them or they spend money on the wrong thing. Modern magnanimous man would spend money even more readily for the non-material than for "things." This is far beyond Marcus Aurelius's dictum of *In medio stat virtus*. It contains the notion of a leadership and love that gives itself entirely to the other. This kind of "propagating" is only possible for true magnanimous men and women. This total going out to others by the leaders, in turn, makes possible the creative relationship, which is the heart of the community.

28

What we are confronted with today in democratic structures of relationship, is a struggle which seems to center around means of communication whereby the leader is convalidated in such a way that it is a noble thing for him to be the leader. Such communication should give him convalidation if he is truly endowed with qualities of leadership. These qualities would give fulfillment to the followers since both choosing and then following a genuine leader are themselves redemptive. A genuine leader can give magnificence and magnanimity to the group which the group by itself might not have. This is what is redemptive to all in leadership that "propagates" itself by going out totally to others. This establishes a creative dynamic for each, that is incarnately redemptive. Such a community gives each person a sense of "being bought with a great price," of being of genuine worth in his whole psychosomatic person. He is of worth not for what he "ought" to be but for what he truly "is."

# II. Celibacy as Authentic Communication

WE wish here to look freshly at "celibacy" from a propagation model but with the direction of the propagation as away from oneself and one's loins and totally out to others. Seen this way, celibacy, applied to both men and women, symbolizes a love totally for others, the model and direction of all love—a love beyond. Unless celibacy in some way symbolizes and does this, it is sterile and meaningless.

Authentic communication, then, of whatever sort, is initiated by this kind of loving—of going out to the other with no sense of return. This would be unconditioned propagating of self, the spreading of oneself out for others, the diffusion of oneself. Celibacy would simply be one model of this kind of creative self-giving.

Basic to our discussion of celibacy, then, will be the notion of community as determined by degrees of communication which grow out of communion. Whatever may be used as a modality of the community, even if it be the city, as Augustine's "City of God," the model cannot hold together unless there is communion within it. Unless there is a genuine authentic communication going on within the community, and that as a result of this communication, there is a sense of communion, the community itself will fail to convalidate and redeem its members. No matter how much structure one may build up

30

around it, and no matter how much power-force is present in the community, at best it can be little more than power-centered, rather than providing the real communion experience that is an essential characteristic of any authentic community.

Authentic communication would bring about some type of redemptive communion in which each person is genuinely convalidated in the Pauline sense of having been "bought at a great price." One's intrinsic value is basic not only to loving himself and to his own sense of worth, but also to his capacity to give himself as a precious gift to others. Whatever definitions one uses for community, they are all measured by, and indigenous to, each person's deepest sense of wanting to belong to an authentic community.

The dynamic sense of whatever people are engaged in must serve as a redemptive process of communion together. In the opposite sense of this, people have often been victimized in our present structures by an *ex*communication experience. While many people may have experienced psychological *ex*communication and *ex*communion, it may be that they have rarely experienced psychological communication or communion. Contained in this notion is the meaning of authentic celibacy.

## APPROACH TO CELIBACY

We will consider celibacy not from the usual theological approach, then, but rather from a fundamentally psychological or dynamic viewpoint. The issue that we are concerned with is the type of authentic communication that celibacy has to offer. What do celibacy and marriage engage people in as a way of living together, and what is effective in that communication? There is no point in holding on to something if it is no longer of any real value.

31

Consequently, celibacy must be looked at in a living, dynamic meaning to determine its value for the present time. It will be necessary to avoid any past fixations around this question and to do so celibacy must be seen as contributing to an authentic dynamic relationship between people. When it is seen this way, the question of marriage or non-marriage becomes less significant.

## LINGUISTIC STEREOTYPES

To see this more clearly, it is necessary to move away from some of the verbal and linguistic stereotypes that, either consciously or unconsciously, a suggestion of the word "celibacy," as well as the word "virginity," has for so many people. There is a certain negation and a feeling of isolation about these words. To make any positive statement about celibacy seems often to imply contradictory and negative things about marriage. Without realizing it and without intending it consciously, a message is usually communicated to the hearer to the effect that marriage is being judged. It is consequently most difficult to speak of celibacy in a free and relaxed way.

Therefore, to clarify and get a fresh look at the word "celibacy," one may be helped by considering the German meaning. The German word for celibacy, "*Ehelos*," is an interesting word in that it simply means marriageless, or the state of not being married. So perhaps it might be simpler to speak about the state of the non-married. This would avoid all the broad and subtle implications that might still be crowded into our psychological "bag" around the notion of celibacy or virginity. Suppose, then, that we talk about the marriageless state or the state of the non-married. This, it seems, will be psychologically helpful insofar as it can then provide a certain relaxed feeling.

For example, one might speak as relaxedly about a

non-married person as he would about a non-smoker. When we speak about the non-smoker there is a fairly relaxed communication while at the same time there is no fear of any indictment or any denegration concerning the smoker. This is simply to say that celibacy is a conscious or unconscious factor in one's life, just as non-smoking would be. If one happens to have a plan of life that does not involve smoking, then when he does not smoke a cigarette, the other person does not necessarily speak or feel negatively about him; it is simply assumed that he has a different way of life.

Something of this relaxed tone in talking about the non-married state can be helpful. It is seen as a way of life for various practical reasons, somewhat analogous to the perhaps conscious way a person, as a young man, never started smoking and so he does not smoke now. So if one says that he does not smoke, there is no great issue; and if he does smoke, this makes no great difference either. But certain things follow as a way of life to one who does not smoke, and other things follow as a way of life to one who does smoke. We might talk about non-married people in that same context, not being distressed about the word "non-married."

## ORDINARY NORMS MISLEADING

Psychologically one precise thing must be faced, however; non-marriage does in fact differ somewhat from the relaxed tone of non-smoking, for there is no question that from a developmental point of view, marriage is one of the things that marks a kind of transition to maturity. Ordinarily we regard it as the mark of an adult when he is thinking about, or approaching, marriage. When one talks about non-marriage, then, it does pose this issue, namely, what happens in the developmental process that causes a person not to marry?

33

If this matter is looked at psychologically, it presents a very real issue which has been one of the difficulties for psychological studies of seminarians. According to the norm of the ordinary population, whether it be the ordinary college population or the ordinary graduate school population, seminarians who are tested by those same norms rate as "abnormal" in the areas of psychosexual development. So unless this obvious conscious variable is introduced which is only applicable to seminarians—they consciously chose a non-smoker's life, that is, they consciously chose to be non-married—it is in the distribution of the population of smokers that non-smokers are comparatively rare.

If one views smoking or, in this instance, marriage as a process from the immaturity of adolescence to the maturity of an adult, then on that norm alone one would rate the non-married as immature. But it seems that this can be handled without any great anxiety and it has been handled that way in the pragmatic solution. To use our analogy of smoking, one might choose celibacy just as one might choose not to smoke; it is simply a pragmatic choice. If one chooses the priesthood, for example, since there are at present certain conditions that he would have to renounce in the Western Church in connection with this choice, his maturity or immaturity is not measured by his not getting married. Where there are very small numbers of men, by comparison to the whole population, consciously choosing, in a pragmatic sense, to be non-married because, in the present case, it fits the structure of the priesthood, that would represent a valid option.

But again it is important to be overtly honest here and face the fact that a choice of celibacy is an issue which, if consciously faced and explicitly looked at, will be the wiser thing, while any attempt to suppress it might be its greatest danger. It is possible, and in some instances probable, that in practice the attraction to celibacy is one that has some type of social abnormality about it. In that sense, therefore, it is necessary to look genuinely at all the other aspects that celibacy entails, because merely being attracted to celibacy alone could be a way of being attracted to a state of not committing oneself to another adult of the opposite sex. This would be evidence of a psychological immaturity and an escapist tendency from genuine committments with other persons.

One might consider a justification of the non-married state by other more profound evidences of real communication together. Celibacy, if seen as a kind of magic fetish, would rightly be regarded as immature and, considered from a psychological scale, quite definitely out of the norm. There is currently a struggle going on among psychologists between a normative approach and a quite pragmatic and statistical view of man which sees him as he is, as we experience him, and not necessarily in any kind of idealistic form.

## IDEALS: BASIC TO THE HUMAN CONDITION

Through a mythological process the human condition expresses certain aspirations which are pragmatically meaningful even though the people themselves might never arrive at these aspirations. For example, if one considers the Sunday afternoon bowling alley, it is statistically evident that the average score is around 140. Such a score is way below the ideal norm of 300, and certainly below the highest scores of 250 or 260 that men in a bowling league would achieve. And yet the aim in the game of bowling is to get a strike every time, and if not a strike, a spare. While a perfect score of 300 is not impossible in a rare instance, it is precisely the aspiration to achieve a score of 300 that makes people want to continue bowling.

So even if one only gets a score of, say, 140, he will keep striving for that theoretical strike in each action. This suggests that if one takes away an ideal aspiration, he removes much of the motivation by which the person got 140. It is the aspiration that inspires the constant struggle to continue. This is seen in many pragmatic situations where one is continually striving to imitate the professional.

## THE AUTHENTIC HERO

This brings us to the place of the hero. The hero of the myth is the aspiration-realizer who acts out for the rest of people what they would all like to be but cannot be. The heroes of sports, for example, are often the living embodiment of what we would all like to be. This is the dynamic of the myth where there is a great fulfillment projected out onto the hero. Because the hero is able to perform so expertly, there is some vicarious fulfillment in each person who witnesses the performance.

A more obviously entertaining type of myth, one that better fits the Greek notion of the hero, is the myth of the American cowboy. If one considers the cowboy myth, he will notice that the cowboy-hero takes a definite form: he is always in some way a redemptive person, not in the manner of the Greek gods, but in the form of the hero-clinician. The word "clinician" is etymologically derived from "incline," that is, the hero is one who "bends down." In our terms, he would be an incarnate or redemptive figure. He is not the hero up among the gods, in the Greek sense; he is more like the Christ-hero. He comes down, he becomes man, he takes upon himself the body of a man, he incarnates himself with people.

In the cowboy myth, the hero rides into town out of nowhere. He comes into a place that is overwhelmed by evil and anguish. It is the non-redeemed town, the town in darkness. The hero comes and through the power of his heroic qualities and through his clinical and incarnate characteristics, he incorporates himself humanly with the people. He takes the side that is being surrounded by evil and through his redemptive powers he redeems the town.

In one phase of this myth he marries the town belle who, in our myth sense, is a kind of goddess, and settles down among the people. In another and equally popular form of this myth, however, he does not marry but rather he leaves the town, riding off alone with the implication that the next episode will find him in another town in a similar situation. This is seen, for example, in popular television serials. There is much repetition of the redemptive process where it seems to be always continuing rather than being closed off by the hero marrying and settling down in the town.

What one sees, therefore, in the myth is a certain level of aspiration, but he sees it realized in someone else. He sees in his hero-clinician what he stands for. The novel or the movie *Shane* seems to be an exact illustration of the cowboy myth. The hero of this novel, Shane, enters the town and deeply incorporates himself with the husband and wife, as seen through the eyes of an eleven-year-old boy. In the story Shane goes through the "sacrificial" act, that is, he sacrifices himself for the husband and wife and the boy and in so doing he is profoundly loved by all three. The wife at one point asks Shane why he is going to perform this sacrificial act, risking his life with the gun-slinger in the local saloon. Shane's answer is that of the redemptive hero: "I am not doing it just for you, I am doing it for all three of you." The hero in this case always holds the husband, wife, and child together, rather than separates them, and the final point of the myth is that of the

37

wounded hero, Shane, riding off into the darkness when the sacrificial redemptive act is performed.

What does such a myth say about the human condition? It seems to suggest some need to see a completed state in the hero. The human race never seems to tire of witnessing a redemptive act, a hero-clinician entering into a situation and giving it wholeness, taking upon himself, not marriage, but the responsibility of restoring to the people their sense of dignity and goodness and leaving them with the memory of him. He is then incarnately redemptive in their eyes, always with the element of wanting nothing for himself. Any talk about maturity presupposes that one person goes out to another. If one attributes some special eminence to himself simply because he is not married, it would be as nonsensical as attributing some kind of magic to oneself simply because he does not smoke. What is important therefore is not whether one is married or whether he smokes or not, but the quality of communication which enables him to arrive at a genuine relationship with others. Celibacy can stand for this authentic going out.

## THE MEANING OF PERSON

It is noteworthy that Augustine must have learned a great deal from the early Christian communities about genuine relationships because what he says is surprisingly modern in the psychological sense. It is much like the clinical experiences that are being witnessed in relationships in therapy and in counseling where one sees the need for deep understanding. Scholars have attributed to Augustine the origin of the rich meaning of the word "person" that we now have. Up to the time of Augustine, "person" was a title in Roman law, as well as a character that "sounded through" a mask, in other words, it was a masked character, a dead, static thing. However, Augustine gave to this word a dynamic meaning that still perdures in all the meaning that is now put into the word "person." He saw in a human relationship something that was incarnately redemptive and which gave great dignity to being a person. It was around this notion that he could use the word "person" and give it such attributes as were finally associated with the godhead.

It is here that the real notion of communication is seen. It is the person's freedom, under certain conditions, to go out and to be genuine with others that creates the incarnately redemptive relationship. The going out is always something new and fresh because there is always an element of risk in it. For example, in talking to circus people, they will say that the most exciting act, and the one that they never tire of, is the one with the greatest risks—the trapese act. This may be so because it so dramatically illustrates the human condition. If one person goes out to another, the great risk is whether that person will "catch him" or not. There is that anxious moment when the one trapeze artist reaches out and grasps the hands of the other so that he does not fall.

This seems to contain the heart of a deep communication. One person trusts the other enough to risk himself to that person. And the other is *logos* enough, in the most profound sense of an understanding heart, to reach the other at the level of his fears and his creature-anxieties, the level of the things that he knows are so "ungodly" in himself and the things for which the god-part of himself condemns him. In the relationship of trust, one does not have to use the mask; rather he risks himself to the other and the other understands him at the deepest level of his incarnate anxiety. Out of this communication of the two comes a profound healing; it is a therapeutic process. It is interesting to note that Augustine used the word "therapy" for "grace." He seemed to understand grace primarily as we now understand therapy. Grace would be a "gracious" kind of thing because it would flow. It would be healing because one person has trusted the other and given to him his unconditioned, incarnate, redemptive uniqueness. Theologically, this would be the spirit of grace, the spirit of gracefulness in its natural form.

In trying to embody this concept, we might use the Narcissus myth. While the Narcissus myth is a simple story, even a kind of fairy tale, it could be quite frightening if one were to understand it thoroughly. Briefly, the myth is this: Narcissus looks into the pool, which serves as a mirror, and he falls in love with the image that he sees there. In this myth what is often forgotten is that Narcissus actually believes that he is in love with another. This is the heart of the myth and if it is overlooked, one misses the real message. The terrifying thing is that Narcissus does not know that the image in the pool is an image of himself and not of someone else. But Narcissus, in reaching out to embrace the other, the image of himself that he sees in the pool in order to experience the other, is cursed by the gods; the object of his love disappears.

The frightening thing is that one can go through life being very convinced that he loves others and never know that he really never tries to experience love. Because he may be afraid to experience it, he remains in the narcissus-image that he is actually loving another. When he tries to experience love he destroys the other person because, in fact, he "eats him up" with his own needs. Even though he may be deeply convinced in his own perception that he loves the other, the deception always remains.

Another aspect of this myth is that Echo actually loved Narcissus, but the tragedy was that Echo could not reach him. Echo was, in a very profound sense, feminine; she was a truly listening heart. But Echo could not "spond," she could only "respond." Narcissus was so caught in his own image that he could not turn to Echo and say, "I love you"; but if he had done so then Echo could have said back, "I love you." Narcissus therefore could never get out of the bind that he was in with the person whom he thought he loved but whom he could not experience. This left Echo completely helpless, then, in any attempt to communicate her love back to Narcissus, because she could only respond to love; Narcissus had to "spond" first.

One of the misleading modern myths that we have been somewhat victimized by is that of a search for simple solutions to life. One of the simplest solutions, for example, came out of World War II and is most successfully dramatized by one of the musical comedies of the time, namely, *South Pacific*. This story portrays the myth of the redemptive element in mere contact with another. Think of the words of the song, "There is nothing wrong here that can't be cured by putting him near a . . . dame."*

It is a winning myth, especially when one makes it "an enchanted evening." The redemptive figure is seen "across the crowded room." But consider the redemptive figure. If one thinks that the gates to redemption are narrow, he might ponder the danger of this myth. It says, "Make her your own or live your life alone." The deception is that somewhere "across the crowded room," there is redemption, no matter what agony of soul the person is in, no matter what kind of torture he is in. If one can only find the redemptive person "across the crowded room," all his aspirations will be answered.

This is wrapped up in a very beautiful form, in a kind of mysticism of marriage, which is psychologically primitive. It suggests that all the agonies of adolescence, all the

*Quoted with permission of Chappell and Company, New York.

41

agonies of loneliness and indignation of life, that come with growing up and that are concomitant with becoming an adult, will somehow or other be magically solved if one can only find this other person.

There is a kind of theological mysticism about it, however, and one might say that marriage was used in this way by the mystics. But it was understood by them as marriage to God. They saw marriage as containing the embryo of total fulfillment but only if it was considered a divine marriage. It is well known that the mystics used marriage as a modality of a final state of communion between soul and God. The difficulty is that we are now trying to put all this divine mystical fulfillment on to one person, the person that one marries.

Some time ago a study was done of five hundred married couples of upper-middle-class status.* What was discovered was that real communication among these five hundred couples, where one would expect to find some of the best marriages, was almost non-existent statistically. Among them alienation existed as deeply as it does in any other group in any walk of life. The point is that there is no magically "enchanted evening" that restores one's ability to go out of himself to someone else.

Another interesting fact was discovered through the study. Insofar as there were any deep communicative relationships among these people, it most often was not between husband and wife. The real communication that existed came about between people who worked together. This is seen, for example, in the boss-secretary myth, or in the doctor-nurse myth. It is these myths that suggest a real

*John F. Cuber, and Peggy B. Harroff, "The More Total View: Relationships Among Men and Women of the Upper Middle Class," in *Marriage and Family Living,* 25, No. 2 (May, 1963), p. 67.

communication between men and women that is not found in marriage.

If it is assumed that marriage will automatically bring about communion and communication, we are seriously misleading ourselves. And likewise, if one imagines that celibacy is going to restore all our relationships with other people, he is caught in another myth. This is a kind of magic or security-blanket.

## NARCISSISTIC PROJECTION

As we suggested, maturity would mean going out to others. The question here is whether marriage achieves this and the obvious answer seems to be that of itself it does not. It seems to offer no advantage as far as enabling a person to go out of himself. On the contrary, and this seems to be repeatedly evident, one of the most painful experiences for married people is to be made aware of the fact that in marriage there can be even extreme narcissistic manipulation between husband and wife, and perhaps even more so between parents and children. If there is any one difficulty that dominates the counseling of college students, it is of their overwhelming sense of trying to free themselves from the narcissistic bind that parents put them in.

Parents can project out onto the children their own unfulfilled needs and in doing so they control the children narcissistically. The result of this is that the college student, or the high school student, will say again and again, "I have no life of my own." "They just squeeze everything out of me." Far from offering a solution to this problem, marriage, then, can bring about a deception in a narcissistic way. Married people often become very skilled in the way that they manipulate one another and their children. One might say that communication can be made more difficult by marriage and the solution to communication is not found simply in the person that one has met on that one "enchanted evening."

## THE CLERGY AND MARRIAGE

Another practical question can be raised here. Insofar as one might see marriage and working together as an ideal, could it be possible that a married relationship would, in fact, aid the work of the clergy. It is obvious that one does not have to go far to study this question. One could look for a moment at a study of married clergymen. What does it show? What is their life condition? The study referred to is one by Daniel D. Walker.* These are his conclusions from a large distribution of Protestant clergymen: It is shown that clergymen are fundamentally no different than very occupied businessmen or medical men. They are often guilt-ridden about having neglected their wives and children. The problem is further complicated. They often feel that they are not free to give themselves to their families as good fathers should. They are with them bodily but not in spirit.

This is not to say anything negative about marriage. It is merely to say that there is no magic in marriage. Marriage will have the same complexities for the clergyman as it has for the doctor, lawyer, and all others. If this study were to be extended, it might be seen that a great many clergymen could be guilty about the neglect of their wife and children because of their prior commitment.

We can consider a further question now. Suppose that the clergyman and his wife were working together in a genuine relationship. Does this fact hold up in the long

*Daniel D. Walker, *The Human Problems of the Minister*, New York, 1960.

run? Apparently it does not. In another study of five thousand ministers' wives, this is what was found:

Of the almost five thousand ministers' wives who filled out questionnaires in this study, about one in five reported themselves to be teamworkers with their husbands. About three in five were in the middle. And slightly less than one in five, if not resistant, were no more involved than if they were in another vocation.*

It is seen from this that if a person is lucky, he has a one-in-five chance to find fulfillment in that relationship. What this comes down to once again is that there does not seem to be any magic either in being celibate and "having it made," or in being married and "having it made."

The issue is back to our general statement: The genuineness that we communicate in relating to one another is based on the authenticity of the communication that one has with himself, whether he is married or celibate. The degree to which one can relate to himself determines in a marked degree how he will relate to others. This would show the great value of counseling in counseling-therapeutic concepts for the work in the life of the unmarried or married person. If it is an issue, not of states in life, or of how we live but of the basic dynamism with oneself, then how one relates with himself will predetermine how he goes out to others.

## CELIBACY VS. THE DEATH-IMPULSE

Celibacy can be seen from a new point of view by going back to the aspiration myth. It is striking that in the Old Testament celibacy, or virginity, was seen as a negative thing; a kind of death-impulse. It had its main positive meaning as a commentary on the transiency of life. For

*William Douglas, *Ministers' Wives*, New York, 1965, p. 46.

45

example, Jeremiah is probably the outstanding illustration of a man who demonstrates celibacy as part of his prophetic mission as a means of representing the beyond. Modern psychological studies are being more and more concerned with the issue of death. They are proposing that unless we can consciously and overtly face death we are not mature.

But note that this is quite a different notion of what psychological maturity is. It is quite different from the popular ideas. The heart of psychological maturity is to confront death constructively. This is more subtle than it may appear. It rather means that loving, the genuine loving of another, is a kind of death. That is to say, unless one is willing to give himself up, which is a kind of dying, he never really experiences love. In a way, Narcissus could not die to himself and so he was hopelessly in his bind. But could he have died to himself he might have been able to turn and tell Echo that he loved her because he would have been able to go out of himself.

One does not love another by imposing his life-forces on them. This merely forces the other to oppose him defensively with his own life-forces, in place of any deep communication. The *logos* contains the implication of genuinely dying to oneself, because to hear the other requires a willingness to die to oneself in order for the other to get through. Thus the listener becomes a kind of other self of the person to whom he is listening. The basis of the whole counseling skill centers around the degree to which the listener can become another self for the speaker. This enables the speaker genuinely to commune with himself through the listener. But in order for this to happen the listener must literally die to himself.

There is something intriguing about the Christian paradox that through dying one lives. One who saves his life in the narcissistic sense, loses it. But insofar as one gives himself over to death willingly, in the sense of losing that dynamic need to oppose others with his life-force, somehow he finds a new redemption in love. He experiences a love far beyond that narrow urge of narcissism where he was deceptively leading himself away from true communion.

Celibacy seems to be a form of this kind of death. The very nature of celibacy is to cut off the life-stream. The celibate, indeed, has no inheritance. Celibacy, in this sense, is one of the noblest self-confrontations and a symbol of living with one's own death-needs. But in the context here, death is a kind of loving and unless one can die he cannot love. This is the Christian paradox.

## Surrogate Reassurance

In attempting to escape that aspect of life which is death, assuming that the core of all man's anxieties with life is his fear of death, man is running away from life. In a surrogate way he is reassuring himself because he cannot face death. It can be seen from this that marriage too offers some surrogates here. A man can feel that he has not too much meaning in his own life, that he is not of too much worth, but he has his children in whom he can really find meaning and significance. This is readily seen as representing the danger of the narcissistic bind—how a man can project out onto his children his own meaning and significance as we have previously noted. He can thus get a certain surrogate meaning from his children and from his grandchildren. Somehow or other, in this way his life has meaning, not in itself, but in others. But celibacy, in an absolute sense, cuts this off. It allows no such rationalization through children or grandchildren. It dramatically says that either the person must "make it" here or he does not "make it"; he either "makes it" through the instrumentality of himself or he fails. He does not have the same rationalization that others have, namely, that if he fails, someone else will succeed for him. He must go out to others.

## DECEPTIVE OPENNESS

We come now to consider the quality of openness which all of this seems to suggest. If one holds himself back and dies to the other, which comes about when one person tries truly to understand another, the other experiences a kind of fulfillment in the understanding person. Many people have recently realized that, while going through the façade of committing themselves to poor people or to handicapped people, for example, the whole commitment can still be fraudulent. At bottom it can be very condescending. This may be where the racial issue has helped us so much. It might be that those who are born to a middle-class home—and this would include all the clergymen in the studies we now have—have the feeling that they have already "made it," because they were born to it. This is the general profile of the priest; he was born with a genetic stream that gives him above-average intelligence. He went to a neighborhood school which was, by definition, a better school. He went on to college because his parents could afford to pay for it. And because of all this he then became a priest or clergyman. But there is in this life a kind of enclosure, a kind of success in "having it made" that renders extremely difficult any genuine approach to the poor. The clergyman cannot communicate on this level of poverty because it is not indigenous to him. There is a basic incommunicability here.

The person who, as a middle-class product, tries to go to the inner-city and to say that he is really sharing the life of the poor can in fact put himself in an increasingly deceptive position. It could be suggested that there is no way out of this, that this is Sartre's *No Exit;* that there is no way into the poor. From this view, it is simply fraudulent to stand on the outside and pretend that one is in, or is even trying to get in.

## COMMUNICATION THROUGH HANDICAP

But let us look at another possibility. Maybe in a subtle way that we do not yet grasp, standing before people with a conscious handicap, like the eunuch, we arrive at the core of the loss of what every man and woman wants. This man or woman standing before the handicapped person, cut off from a natural life-principle, willingly stands for something that includes the handicapped in a love relationship where the basic need and drive for children is willingly forfeited.

It may be that this is a most profound kind of communication. It could say to me that when I really believe that this is what you are, you, the celibate, love no one more than me, you are committed to no one more than me. In this moment of time you can give me your whole self; you can die that I may live through you because you are not committed to anyone else. You can make that gift honestly and openly because there is no one else on your mind who receives priority, as a wife, husband, or children might.

It is a witness of this loving openness to others which seems essentially to be the cutting off of oneself to let the other in, and having cut off oneself so that the other may get through, one communicates an openness to the other. In few other ways could a person communicate with another and not be condescending; but he can stand before another as a man genuinely cut off from his own life-impulses that the other may live through him. And his glory and his meaning will be another kind of life through

49

others which has to be genuine because he has nothing else.

The celibate, therefore, propagates by allowing others to come to life in and through him because he is willing to die to a basic aspect of himself for them. The great challenge of our generation is to work out how we can be genuinely and incarnately redemptive to one another. This will be accomplished not simply by having heroes "up there," and projecting redemption on to them, assuming that they will save us. Rather creative communication that convalidates each of us must come from a special and unique way of caring for one another. Celibacy could symbolize one aspect of this genuine kind of real caring.

# III. The Church as Person

OUR basic theme thus far has been authentic communication. The focal point has been the notion that a community is impossible without a concept of communion. Consequently, the stress has been on the notion of community in a wide variety of applications. Moving now to a broader spectrum of the conceptualization of community we are confronted with a conception of the Church itself.

## NON-LINGUISTIC COMMUNICATION

Our consideration of the Church might be introduced by a discussion of psycho-linguistics. Psycho-linguistics is a development of an older conception known as semantics. What is of great value in the study of linguistics is the degree to which we are able to penetrate to various levels of the meaning of a word. As will be seen, this is important for a discussion about the Church. In penetrating the subtleties of the meaning of a word, and therefore in penetrating the subtleties of communication, linguistic research has brought out the awareness that we often speak to one another on two or more levels of linguistic and non-linguistic communication simultaneously. Thus a person may be saying two or three things while linguistically he appears to be saying only one.

For example, a person might be speaking on an affective and on a cognitive level at the same time. To illustrate this fact, if one were to ask a person to react spontaneously to the word "candy," he might give a positive affirmation about the word. But there could also be a negative response if the person does not like candy or, for instance, if he is on a diet. But in either case we see this word involving the person in a subtle emotional operational system. Thus if one goes into the feeling world he sees that the word "candy" has a double layer of meaning.

To become more specific still, one might take a phrase such as "chocolate covered cherries," and he may see a negative reaction if the person has become sick on this kind of candy at some time in the past. But the reaction might not necessarily be a nauseating one; it could be a visual-tactile one if the person had gotten "goo" on himself at one time. One can see, then, that a given word has different resonances and repercussions for different people that may go back into their past history and might be expressed in a moment of positive or negative reaction.

## THE PSYCHO-LINGUISTIC MEANING OF "CHURCH"

This example illustrates that a word may have various levels of subtlety distinct from the conscious, logical, apparent meaning of the word. It can be helpful, therefore, to try to see some of the overtones and undertones that the word "church" implies. Various concepts of the Church, too, carry an unconscious and implicit "value package" which may predetermine the kind of reaction one has and even why he reacts without being consciously aware of it. "Package" indicates what a word like "Church" can have wrapped up or in its "bag." When we use the word "Church," it may contain aspects that will entangle us, and unless we can disentangle ourselves from all the hidden meanings of this word, we could become highly victimized in what we are trying to do. We could

52

become entrapped by the "package" that is "wrapped" up in the word "church."

It seems that there are actually two packages which, in their complication, affect us. One is a fairly obvious one, and can be dismissed quickly. There is an element that is historically tied up with militarism around the word "church." The military application to the church largely comes from military analogies that, in a simple way, were contained in the New Testament. There the church was seen in some sort of battle array and a certain concept of warfare pervaded it. But presented from a psycho-linguistic point of view, as these military words appear in the New Testament, they are seen as rather innocuous. There are many other analogies of the Church equally picked up from the experiences of the people of the time. Thus one need only look at the analogical meaning of the use of "battle" in the Scriptures.

The military and psycho-linguistic unconscious structure related to the Church was brought to a far greater historical significance by the long period of the crusades, and this was perhaps retained somewhat by the Papal States later on. The Roman Church actually emerged to become a kind of military force, and in consequence, it increasingly became identified with a particular area of Europe called the Papal States. Thus the Pope, in some sense, would have represented an actual military leader.

It is probably not an excessive exaggeration then to say that in the word "church" historically, as it has grown psycho-linguistically, there is the suggestion of a military force, or a military structure. The Church as a military force, like the Crusades, is so obviously what we now see that the Church should not be, that this notion can be discharged quite easily once one is conscious of it.

The other conception that is suggested to us by the

53

word "church" is one which, in its first awareness, is glorious and magnificent. But before we go into this we might first consider an awareness from counseling and psychotherapy that can be helpful in seeing the process of conceptual change. Psycho-linguistics is related to insight in the therapeutic and counseling change because personal struggle for self-awareness often results in the same kind of enriching penetration into the past and arriving at different meanings for words.

At some point in the life of the child he congeals on a certain feeling tone around a parent figure. Therefore, ever after that if one were to ask a child anything about his family, he might spontaneously talk a great deal about his mother and say very little about his father; or he might alternately say a great deal about his father and very little about his mother. From a semantic viewpoint the term "mother," when he says very little about his mother, has congealed in a somewhat negative tone of which he may not be consciously aware. But the negative tone is revealed in the very fact that he does not talk very much about his mother, whereas the term "father," congealed in a positive resonance of tone, is very exciting to him.

## PSYCHO-LINGUISTIC AWARENESS

Using this awareness from the counseling process, what might happen to the psycho-linguistic relationship of a person with his father or his mother? He might slowly begin to realize that while he has been quite openly hostile to his father, his more mature, rational judgment of himself reveals that he was more positive towards his mother for less than valid reasons. While the mother gave in to him and did many things for him, in another sense she really did not care that much about him. In a way she was only dismissing him by being kind and by giving him presents, for example. But as he looks back now at his

54

father, even though he was linguistically reacting to him negatively, he now maturely begins to see that the giving in of the mother was a way of forcing the father to be harsh and stern. The more profound thing that he may begin to see is that the father really cared about him and was harsh and stern not necessarily because he wanted to be that way, but actually because he cared about him. The father realized that the boy needed some kind of discipline, the more so because of the leniency and the manipulation of the mother.

Within this psycho-therapeutic process a psycho-linguistic change is occurring also. Somewhere along the line the person begins to react positively to the term "father" and much less superficially positive to the term "mother." He has much more depth now in response to both of these terms. This, then, is a kind of psycho-therapeutic process that is also psycho-linguistic in regard to the terms "father" and "mother." What is seen to have happened is that processes of changed awareness, as the person is looking again at his own life, have taken place in him.

It is not, then, so much that the people we blame, such as our father or our mother, for our fixations on the past, have been "bad"; rather, it is more a matter of them having reacted as best as they could to the circumstances of the time. For example, a person's mother might have been over-solicitous for him when he was a child. But perhaps her need to be that way was that the child was very sickly, perhaps nearly dying on one or other occasion. Consequently, the mother simply responded to the sickly condition of the child by great solicitude. But when the child becomes older, and through the psycho-therapeutic and psycho-linguistic process he comes to see how it was in the past between himself and his mother, he can then change in his attitude towards her. He can respond to the term "mother" much more positively as he now recognizes that although his past relationship with his mother may have caused him certain difficulties, these are now no longer relevant or important. As a mature person he has his separateness and independence from her. He does not reject her, but simply understands that the passage of time has made his relationship with her different. He has changed his whole image with regard to her and to his father. The result is a more mature relationship, especially with the father.

## PSYCHO-LINGUISTIC CHANGE

We might now try to relate this process to the meaning of the Church. What seems to be happening in the historical process that we are going through is similar to the counseling-psycho-therapeutic and psycho-linguistic process. As people begin to question, as they have over a period of time, the structure and the meaning of the Church, we see a similarity to the way a person begins to question the structure of his own life in his past and in his present. People begin to see that there were many strange and conflicting aspects that, through their experience in the Church, are no longer relevant.

What seems to be implied here is that all the "binds" that the word "church" implies are still operant but are no longer helpful. We can be helped a great deal psycho-linguistically, however, by a sharper awareness of what these restrictions seem to be implying, somewhat like the change in concept towards the meaning of the word "mother."

## THE HISTORICAL MODALITY OF THE CHURCH

About the time of Charlemagne new traces of Western Civilization as we now know it began to appear. While we

56

know relatively little about Charlemagne himself, one of the things that seems to be historically true is that he read Augustine's *City of God* and was dominated by the idea that it contained. As a result, he was drawn to incorporate into the Holy Roman Empire something of the splendor and glory that was the City of God. This move turned out to be very effective. The image that followed from his time into the twelfth, thirteenth, and fourteenth centuries is an image that the Church is not simply a religious organization, not simply a place where people pray, not simply where they learn about and experience religion, but that it is a powerful civilizing force. The purpose of the Church therefore was to develop a Christian civilization.

One might note especially the word "civilization." The French word *"civiliser"* is the highest expression that can be used for a cultured and sensitive man. The linguistic meaning is evident throughout the whole development of the Church. Thus we see the Church viewing itself as an instrument of civilization. Therefore, the model of the city was the central force that would bring the civilizing processes together. This whole period—the twelfth, thirteenth, and fourteenth centuries—was a glorious period of the modality of the Church as a city, and it might even be suggested that this brought on the Renaissance. The Church was seen as a powerful, civilizing force in the direction of God.

What followed from this was a burgeoning movement that Augustine himself appears not to have realized would ever happen. Somewhere around the time of the Renaissance the "city of man," far from being dead, or barbaric, or simply the force of evil, increasingly took over the civilizing process. It more and more became the magnificent force that carried with it all the great gifts of civilization, such as culture and education. As this process emerged, the different cities began to battle one another, seeing one another as conflicting "cities." Gradually the battleline between the city of God and the city of man seemed to be more clearly drawn. Something of this seems to be what we are facing now. But there is a further complexity: there is no longer the glory and magnificence of the modality of the city, once the city's civilizing character is taken away.

## THE MEANING OF CITY

It seems that the Greeks were the first to understand, at least in the sense of our Western cultural civilization, the meaning of the city. Perhaps one of the greatest tragedies in Western Civilization occurred with the destruction of the Greek city. In some degree, Homer might be considered as representing the loneliness, the longing and the alienation of a civilized man for a city that has been destroyed. There is a prophetic longing in the Greek tradition for a kind of lost city. The Romans later took this up and, around the magnificent city of Rome they incorporated all the ideals in the notion of a city. It might be proposed then that the "City of God" was modeled after the Roman city, that is, the city of Rome.

This has understandably dominated our thinking and it helps to explain how we presently call ourselves Roman Catholics, meaning that we are of the city of Rome. But if one looks closely at the Roman culture that established the city it is seen as a cold, disembodied, rational culture. It has often been pointed out that in the Greek concept of God there is no love, and even less love in the Roman concept of God. What dominated Roman thinking, especially as it was applied to the city, was the notion of law and order. This is illustrated, for example, in Roman architecture. What the Romans wanted to see was a highly ordered kind of civilization. In other words, the prime

element of graciousness and of meaning and of significance in the Roman mind was *order*. And the prime means
by which order was brought about, and the thing the
Romans delighted in most, was *law*. The Roman had a
profound sense of the value of law because he had such an
overwhelming appreciation of beauty as it was contained
in order.

## THE GOSPEL MODELS OF THE CHURCH

No doubt this awareness causes us some concern and
anxiety. If we view the Church in the powerful modality of
the city, we are implying that a hierarchy of values will
give first place to the concept of order, and to bring about
order, law is necessary. Thus when we discover the
Church as it is revealed in the Gospel, we begin to grow
somewhat uncomfortable. The Christian Church of the
Gospels does not seem to be a city, nor does it seem to be
the highly organized process that Rome stood for.

Let us look at the Gospel for the moment. What are the
images of the Church there? They are not the rigid images
of the city; rather, in the Gospel, the Church is many
things, but above all it is a moving, living entity. For
example, the Church of the Gospel is always presented to
us in warm, human analogies. It has much to do with safety
and with danger. But we also get the image, surprisingly
enough, of the Church as a wilderness because, so often,
the thing to do in order to be a Christian in the Gospels is
to leave the safe place, the "ninety-nine" who are not in
need of help and to go out in the wilderness. This conveys
the image of a Church operating in the human region of
alienation and loneliness.

Consequently, any kind of functioning within the
Church is not simply law and order. For example, any
sensible lawyer would know when to walk away from a
situation, and if a reasonable person saw a band of wolves

59

coming for something so relatively valueless as a flock of sheep, the best legal decision in the world would permit him to run away. But the good shepherd, on the contrary, waits and lets the wolves attack him because he loves the sheep. Yet this would appear absurd to the law-and-order-minded Roman.

Seen in this way, the Gospel conception of the Church could not possibly have fit into the smooth and polished imagery of the Roman and Greek architecture. Let us look again at some of the Gospel images. The Church is yeast that is put into bread—note the living, expanding force implied here. In this image there could not possibly be a city of God versus a city of man. How could one put yeast into bread and say that they are separated or that they are in opposition to one another? Even more subtle than this is the analogy of the Church as salt that does not lose its savor. A moment's reflection will reveal that salt, used to cure meat, does not basically change the meat; rather, it penetrates it with a subtle flavor that when one has tasted it, he is especially satisfied and delighted. To describe how salt produces this very desirable flavor in meat is, however, difficult. It is an intangible change that is produced. But anyone who has had the experience of eating well-seasoned meat knows what it tastes like. And anyone who has not had this experience would find it hard to understand any explanation of what salt does to meat. This is the Church, as described in these images. It is equally difficult to describe the subtle flavor that the Church gives to real living. But suddenly every living experience becomes savored by the Christian sensitivity, refinement, fullness, and Christian effulgence.

## CHANGE IN REDEMPTIVE MEANING

What happened that all this was lost? It is apparently not so much that particular attitudes or relationships or

60

THE CHURCH AS PERSON

processes developed later and were wrong in themselves. Indeed the fact that many customs and practices were carried on for such a long time indicates that they must have had some value. But whatever power many such things had, this has finally reached a point of diminishing returns. But a person may still be unconsciously holding on to inadequate models. He will then be unable to devise more dynamic models.

This is what may have happened with the civilizing process of the Church. It was difficult to abandon all that was concomitant with this process. Even now, because of the earlier rich and glorious period, it is hard to let go. It is hard to abandon all its structures and developments.

The redeeming process of the Church, as it developed historically, resulted from penetrating the culture with a great sense of religious and secular achievement. This kind of redeeming sense that the Church brought to man during the Middle Ages lifted him up, elevated him, swept him up like the towering image of Gothic cathedrals. This was its special quality: it permeated civilization with the grace and meaning that gave man a redeemed feeling of special worth.

Consequently, the Church did the one great thing that psychologically a person needs: it gave a sense of personal value. It helped to bring about that realization of St. Paul's words that we are all "bought at a great price." But it did this in a cultural way. It did not do it to individual people. On the contrary, and this was perhaps necessary, the Church never quite became able to disentangle itself from the Greek and Roman structures. The result was that men from the time of Bellarmine and earlier had difficulty with many of these structures. The Church seems to have wanted to hold on to these structures because they are familiar and have been the means to achieving greatness in the past. It felt secure in holding on to a model of society

61

still like the Greek hierarchy which had God on top and below, the lesser gods and goddesses, that is princes and nobles, and down near the bottom are the ordinary human beings.

In this model the ordinary human beings at the bottom should never question those above them. The point of Greek mythology was to keep the general populace in awe and to teach them always to respect those above them. In this the Church was similar to the rest of the culture. The whole class system of England and the continent, even as recently as 1880, was clearly based on a perpetuation of power and strength in the upper class.

## INCARNATE EXCELLENCE

It was through this vertical arrangement that the notion of excellence was conveyed. Excellence was in the *noblesse* while the rest of the human race itself remained, in some sense, children. Only the nobles are adults in this conception. These are the ones who settle the issues of the world. Within that structure of the city, excellence was contained at the top. Worth came not "because I am myself," or because of any special worth in oneself, but because one had received the gracious favors of the elite. The ordinary person, then, was considered a child of not too much importance. The real meaning of the human race was expressed in the phrase *"noblesse oblige."* The nobles were the only ones who had responsibilities. Inherent in this concept of the city is not only the modality of it as a place of law and order; but also the implication that worth and meaning come only from the well-born.

What is happening in our time is that this notion is breaking down. Magnificent as it was, it can no longer sustain man in a purposeful existence. Excellence has become incarnate and has come down to earth. The Greek totem pole is slowly becoming what is essentially the Christian message, namely, that God became man and dwelt among us. For the first time in history a real incarnational relationship is possible.

## CHURCH AS IMAGE OF THE PERSON

While one may see the heavens by looking up, and even pray by looking up, what is also being suggested is a horizontal view. This means that God can be found not only by looking up to heaven but also by looking into the faces of other people. This has finally confronted us all with the most basic element of the Gospel message, namely, how can one love God whom he does not see if he does not love the person next to him?

This is the essential notion of a Christian community. Once we disentangle ourselves from a city image, we come to another meaning of the Church. Our perspectives are changed. Our age is an age of the human person. It is now no longer one's place on the totem pole but the individual person who matters. If this is so, then perhaps the most magnificent image that we can give the Church now is the image of the person.

When the Church is seen as person, we move into the Church as a dynamic human and divine community. In such a community a person must be free to give himself to the other genuinely and openly, in sureness that he can trust the other. His faith in God is validated by his faith in the other person. And the other, deeply sensitive to his needs, responds in deep and warm understanding. Out of this relationship comes incarnate and redemptive love. Excellence, rather than being seen in representation by near God-like figures above us, is contained in the person himself. Equality and excellence are possible together if each one gives and receives profound respect to himself

63

and others as persons. This would be the final validity of the modality of the Church—the Church as person.

This does not mean that the Church should not be clear in its purpose and its need to present its teaching. However, it would be a teaching that is warm and sensitive to the struggle and pain of learning. In this context the word "disciple" most clearly represents the one who is learning, in the literal sense of that word. If the Church is this kind of communion of "persons," then excellence will come from the sense of convalidating worth that emerges each time one person is related to another. We gain our sense of worth in the way that others reflect worth to us. The little child grows to feel worthy in himself in proportion as he is convalidated by people who consider him worthy. One cannot give redemption to himself; another must give it to him. If a person is sufficiently redeemed by others in this way, at some point he will accept and internalize his own sense of worth. Having arrived at a deep sense of his own redemptive worth and intrinsic value, he is capable of going out to and of loving others and so of redeeming them.

## THE CONVALIDATING POWER
## OF THE COMMUNITY

In the Church as a person, dedicated to furthering a sense of personal excellence, we have returned to one of the sources of the Church's earliest strength. One of the reasons why Christianity succeeded so rapidly and so effectively in its early period was that in the large cities, such as Rome, there was a vast inner-city of seemingly worthless and meaningless people. What gave the Christian community in the inner-city its strength was that somehow each of these people was able to give to the others a sense of their real worth and meaning through this community. Because it was such a redemptive community, it spread out and affected the world.

Loneliness, anxiety, and doubt about their own worth seemed also to exist in the early Christian communities. St. Peter gives a graphic description of the early Christian community. He was preoccupied by how transient the world is, how quickly it passes, and he is caught up in the anxiety that is the inheritance of us all. He asks the community not to allow these forces of death to overcome it, not to allow petty jealousies and bickering to get in the way of a genuine going out to one another. We seem to be on the verge of a fresh and new understanding of what St. Peter describes in his first epistle as a "royal priesthood."

One participates in this royal priesthood by not allowing the forces of death to enter, by having one's communication redemptive and convalidating. In proportion as one's communication has become that, he has become a participant in a holy priesthood of the community itself. This suggests that we are moving into a new meaning of ourselves as persons in our understanding of communion and communication as a special way to offer spiritual sacrifice.

We are now beginning to see ourselves incarnately together. Our "royal" quality is emerging in the way that we communicate with one another, in the degree to which we are mutually redemptive. This is not only a priesthood, but it is a royal priesthood. It is the royal priesthood whose loving sacrifices convalidate others in redemptive experience together.

# IV. The Redemptive Community

FOLLOWING from what we have been discussing about the nature of community and the Church as "persons" we can now take up the notion of what a redemptive community might be. One of the most striking descriptions of the process of maturity in the early Christian Church is found in the writings of St. Paul. In the modality of the Christian Church that he uses, we begin our spiritual lives with "milk for babes" and progress to "strong meat for men."

The latter analogy demands strong muscles and developed teeth so that one can tear and rend the food before swallowing it, in contrast to the infantile sucking of milk. St. Paul expresses his disappointment when he says, "I fed you with milk, not solid food, for you were not yet ready for it" (I Cor. 3, 2). He expected a maturity which the Christian community did not have, and he went on to say: "Nor are you ready for it, for you are still carnal" (I Cor. 3, 2). His use of the word "carnal" here would seem to indicate a dependency on him for he had wanted them to move from this dependency to their own integrated ability to live the Christian life without him.

## ORAL MODALITY

Freud has made a great deal of the oral development of the child. Correctly understood, this conceptualization seems applicable to our discussion. We are all oral in various

66

ways. For example, in any type of threat or stress or anxiety, it is satisfying to get something into one's mouth. The early stage of one's development is quite oral in that one needs a great deal of "thing" reassurance. The core of orality is "thingness" and "thingizing." One externalizes his need of security by putting a thing into his mouth and holding on to it.

The notion of "milk for babes" seems to capture this process of development. The milk simply goes into the digestive system in an unanalyzed, uncritical, unresponsive absorption. But in the process of development one grows a set of teeth to chew solid food, to rip it apart. According to the "one receiving," it must be broken down and only then is it digestible in the system. In the dynamic sense of this model, we are talking about a continuum, then, that is a progression from "milk" to "meat."

## NON-COMPETITIVE MODEL

In view of such a living, dynamic model, the question will arise, where have we acquired the static notion of the Christian community? Such a notion seems suggested in the model of the Church as a "city." Within this model it is understandable to pose two cities, the secular city and the City of God, in competition with each other. However, this is a static model which Christ seemed to dismiss. He said, "My kingdom is not here." There seems to be no rival city implied in what He was saying.

We seem to have been trapped in this static model of a rival city, but a truer and more dynamic model of the community is seen where Christ sends the Disciples into the cities (Matt. 10, 5–15). This is the first pragmatic or operant system that describes, in reality, what the Church is. The Disciples were to enter a city and become part of

67

whatever community was there. They were not to stay on the outside of it, nor to set up anything rivaling it, but to enter it.

## EXTENDED EUCHARISTIC PRESENCE

If one looks at the early dynamic Christian community, one of the striking things about it was the sense of sacramentality that pervaded it. The community was itself a sacrament. To focus on water as the key "thing" in Baptism, would be to overlook the person and the community that is baptizing; or to focus on oil in Extreme Unction is to overlook the person and the community that is anointing. This exaggerated focus on the "things" of the liturgy could be thought to represent a "milk for babes" mentality. It is not the "shredding" of the meat and "digesting" it that the mature process of eating involves nor the more mature Christian community that Paul hoped for. Such a notion of mature sacramentality suggests a fullness and fruition of Christianity that we cannot experience if we remain in the "milk for babes" stage.

We are apparently coming from many directions to the awareness of a eucharistic presence that extends out, in and through other people. The modality of the presence of Christ in the Eucharist, as traditionally viewed, is that of nourishment, symbolizing Christ nourishing us with his grace. This, however, can be too easily turned into an oral model which may be abused. If, for example, receiving the Eucharist in communion simply results, in fact, in a preference on the part of the communicant to avoid the human encounter, then this modality is misleading and subject to abuse. In effect, we may be "controlling" God as we do food.

In order to free ourselves from this imagery, the

familiar text of the presence of Christ found in the Gospel of St. Matthew is helpful. It is a text which has been neglected possibly because with our older models we did not know how to deal with it: "Wherever two or three are gathered in my name, there am I in their midst" (Matt. 18, 20). This is also a statement of Christ's Presence in the Christian relationship with other persons. This might be said to be a concomitant result of Christ's presence in the Eucharist itself.

Protestants have seen the key issue here, which is the presence of Christ in human fellowship. Their difficulty, however, has been that they thought "in Jesus' name" signified a kind of special invocation sufficient to bring about Christ's presence. But clearly something much more profound is intended. However, we can use and build on their basic notion of "fellowship." This gives us a foundation for finding the presence of Christ in the Christian community.

We are in no way implying here a diminution of our respect for or our faith in the eucharistic presence under the form of bread and wine. We are stressing an extension of this deep belief and reverence to the whole community and not merely keeping it wrapped up and isolated within each person. In this sense, to "receive communion" must be something more than a passive act. One must initiate the conditions by which Christ is worthily revered and honored in and through each one in the Christian community itself.

We find in the Epistle of St. Peter (I Pet. 2, 9) yet another parallel which, while puzzling, and one which Protestants have also been using, is yet consistent with the entire concept of fellowship. He points out that insofar as we relate openly and "without guile" to one another, we become "living stones" in the body of Christ, and these

69

stones form the altar and the sacrifice of Christ. Thus we have a statement of Christ's presence in the community. St. Peter states that in this way each living stone forms the priesthood of Christ, which he calls, as we saw earlier, a "royal priesthood." He insists on total openness towards one another, and love "without affectation."

## CHRIST IN ONE ANOTHER

Thus we see that a person's realization of Christ comes about not by simply coming to communion and orally receiving the host. After receiving the host, people must somehow invest in and be concerned for one another. For Paul and Peter, to speak of the meaning of Christ without openness and true community seems inconceivable. Paul earlier expressed his disappointment that the Christian community was not yet capable of this "strong meat," this mature responsibility to one another. He had been mistaken in thinking that the people were ready for this mature openness, trust, and responsibility.

Conceivably our whole culture is moving to a point where we can better see Christ in one another. The sacrifice of Christ through bread and wine in the Mass, must result in Christian attitudes and behavior that are not simply a "milk for babes" image but reveal the deep sense of "Look at the Christians; see how they love one another." In this we see indeed a royal priesthood in action! Such an incarnate redemptive relationship contains the deep sense of worth and meaning of each person in the community. Out of this openness and sharing together come a sense of royalty in the truest form.

## THE MEANING OF ROYALTY

Royalty today means little to most people. It is, therefore, important to rethink what royalty meant to St. Peter. It has the sense of a redeemed person. Since we today no longer think in terms of noble figures, "royal" means an incarnate-redemptive worth which we convey to one another. There have been examples of relating nobility to ordinary people in the past. It is said that people of the Basque country at one time conferred nobility on everyone, so that in traveling abroad, they were all eligible to the rights and privileges of nobility. Something of this concept can be applied to each Christian who has been "bought at a great price." We see today that it is important not only that we have gone to communion but also that this increases our sense of Christ's presence in another human person.

## SPACE FOR CHRIST

When one internalizes St. Paul's question, "Know you not that you were bought by a great price?" he walks out of the sacrificial community, not only with holy communion, but with a eucharistic sense of the living Christ that is in each person.

We have to ask what brings about this sense of the royal priesthood. Insofar as we are narcissistically wrapped up in the manipulation and the use of one another, there is no space for Christ to enter. There is no proper "materia" for the presence of Christ in that kind of narcissism. Christ has assured us that He will come under the right conditions, namely, to those who gather "in my name." This seems to imply that His presence can occur between us when one person pulls himself back from manipulating the other so that there is space in between which allows Christ to enter. But there is apparently no way that Christ's promise can be fulfilled if narcissistically we control and manipulate one another. One must contain and control this selfishness and so, in the "loving one another without

71

guile" of St. Peter, the Christian community is convalidated.

In the relationship with another person, Christ's presence is promised in the manner by which this relationship is truly in Christ's name. In proportion as one ceases to use the other for himself there is the possibility of Christ in the midst of the two of them. This is the royal priesthood, literally described, as the Christian community in St. Peter's first epistle. Thus the meaning of sacrifice here would be that one "breaks" himself and so contains himself to let the other enter in. In that breaking, Christ can also enter. In the process of Christian community, the salt will savor the meat with the delicious flavor of such a genuine engagement and authenticity, that one will have no doubt of this special Christian encounter.

## THE PEOPLE OF GOD

The people of God, then, as a community, is related to a royal priesthood. This priesthood is in all the Christian community, in and through the ordained priesthood. The ordained priesthood fuses itself out into the whole community. The life of the ordained priest, therefore, must stand for the priesthood in the lives of the people.

The Greek word *"mimesis"* can be helpful here in defining the role of the ordained priest. It is a word that Plato uses in reference to learning. He makes the point that one learns from another in proportion as one sees the other as representing what he would like to be. For example, if a person speaks perfect German, then he represents what the one learning to speak German would like to be. This creates a mimetic bind between the knower of German and the learner. It does not mean that the knower is necessarily superior to the learner. It simply means that in German the learner would like to be as the knower. This is the mimetic relationship.

The priesthood of the people could then be considered a mimetic relation to the ordained priesthood. The ordained priest must lead in openness to others and in redemptive regard in order to facilitate giving each person in the community a sense of convalidation, of having been "bought at a great price." Each person has reflected his own "royalty" and, therefore, his own redemptive worth. Seen in this Christian way, "royalty" comes about from our free choice to render to one another the kind of worth that is implicit in religious redemption. We are a chosen people of God and we show this in our royal regard as we relate redemptively to one another.

In treating some of the subtleties of the Christian community and the law, St. Paul uses the analogy of the pedagogue. This, like "milk for babes," implies a relationship of dependency that holds only for a time. He is talking about a relationship of decreasing dependency of the learner on the teacher-knower, as the learner internalizes what he gets from the knower-pedagogue. The model is the knower or teacher-learner relationship.

In nearly all discussions of changes in the organizational structure of the Church, the implicit or explicit modality is that we are moving from an absolute monarchy to a democracy. Therefore, we must take certain steps to bring this increasingly about. So the Pope, on the earlier monarch model, should now give more power to the bishops, the bishops, in turn, should give more power to the priests. The priests must then give more power to the people. But this is a focus on power. As long as one is focused exclusively on "the will to power," one has not yet arrived at the conditions of openness that furthers "will to community."

We saw that Christ did not propose that the Church be a city, nor did He consider any such political model of power. In fact, when alternate kingdoms were proposed,

He denied any connection. "Give to Caesar the things that are Caesar's." Insofar as he used the word "royal" or "kingly," He meant it in all the redemptive glory that St. Peter was using it, namely, that we are "royal" insofar as we are elevated and chosen people of God.

## THE TEACHING CHURCH

If we look at the "mission" of the Church then, or what Christians are commissioned to do, we come to something that is both confusing and familiar, depending on how we look at it. "As the Father sent me, I also send you," has the same meaning as St. John's statement that "It is not that we first loved God but that God *first* loved us," and "so should we love one another." In this way, we are "sent," to love first.

There is another element interwoven in this. It is, "Go, teach ye all nations." The Church is then also a *teaching-learning community* in an atmosphere of loving first. If there is a teaching relationship, there must be a knower and there must be learners, and there must be a mimetic process by which learners gradually become like knowers. St. Paul describes this mimetic process in his words, "Be ye *imitators* of me as I am of Christ." He had become so mimetic of Christ that Christ lived in him.

Because of a Cartesian-Kantian distortion in our culture, it has been difficult to see love in the Church as a teaching-learning community. This distortion was based on the notion that man was a pure intellect and a will. In this view, teaching was merely a matter of intellectualizing and factualizing. People either learned or they did not learn. If they did not learn or act on what they learned, they had bad will or a poor intellect or both.

In a city model of the Church, all that basically needs to be taught is the law. That is what the city is for. The city

74

sets down the law, teaches it, promulgates it, and if one is a good citizen or a "good" Christian, that is to say, if he is law-abiding, then he will obey. However, we are proposing that teaching is more than a matter of intellectualizing, factualizing, and issuing an edict. It must involve a mimetic bind between knower and learner in an atmosphere of loving first, of going out to others in redemptive openness.

If we look at learning as a total incarnate and personal experience, involving all the affective as well as the cognitive aspects of man, we do away with the Cartesian-Kantian distortion. In the Cartesian-Kantian model, the knower is superior because, like the city model, he has maximum power. The learner "sits at his feet." He must give back to him what is said but not in an internalized sense of whole-person redemptive communication. Rather it is a "mystery-mastery complex" where the knower holds both superiority and power.

In the redemptive teaching-learning situation, the knower is not superior to the learners, nor are the learners themselves inferior. But the learners make a commitment to the knower. They believe in what he knows; and he, as a responsible knower, struggles to be understanding and understood and to teach. The learners become in a sense the counselor, in that they deeply and sensitively seek to understand him and what he is mimetic to. In the process of so doing, they grow to understand. In this, they increasingly become knowers and more like the knower in what he stands for. This is no vertical model; it is horizontal and mutually fulfilling and redemptive. Unless there are learners who are willing to try to understand the knower, the knower remains isolated and unfulfilled in his knowledge.

In the Christian model, the ordained priests are "sent"

to love, to be open to, to be mimetic to the community. They are the ones who love first. In this they imitate St. Paul. And as the whole Christian community learns from them, it learns how to love one another as they see and experience this in and through the ordained priests.

The ordained priest then is mimetic to the Christian message. He begins by reaching out to others in understanding them. But he, in turn, also needs to be understood, to have his love shared. St. Paul speaks of a longing to share himself with the community. He speaks of being in an *"agonia"* until the members of the community are "born," until they understand him and grow in their own mature Christian faith and independence.

The model of learning here is that the knower must decrease and the learners must increase. In proportion as the knower decreases he loses power, but he gains in the creative sense of seeing other people "born." In proportion as the learner increases, he gains power because he, the learner, less and less needs the knower. At some end point, he—becoming "knower"—then goes out to teach and love first.

## An Incarnate Redemptive Learning Model

If we see the notions of community, communication, communion, and belonging as intrinsic to the educational process, then we are talking about a different educational relationship than a depersonalized knowledge exchange. This is an incarnate redemptive process in which, by becoming incarnate together in recognizing all the feelings and tones of the learning community, both knower and learner are redeemed. The need of both to be understood on the cognitive as well as the affective level is recognized. Insofar as the knower recognizes the intense effort of the learners to understand him, he recognizes a great gift from them. The learner, however, also receives a precious gift in the form of knowledge that he gets from the knower. He becomes like the knower in that which he seeks to know and become.

This is what it means to become Christlike. Christ yearned to convey to men what he knew. He was the knower who loved first. Yearning to be like the knower, the learners commit themselves in their genuine struggle to learn from Him. Christ gave us a model of this teaching-learning process, "No difference is to be made among you, between the greatest and the youngest of all, between him who commands and him who serves" (Luke 22, 12).

The concept of the Church as a teaching-learning relationship, clearly implies a different concept of teaching and learning than our present Cartesian-Kantian model. In our concept of learning as an incarnate-redemptive self-investment process, we are then proposing a change in the model of learning. This change is from an intellectual model or a conditioning model to one borrowed somewhat from the experiences of counseling, psychotherapy, and recent personality theory. We are not thinking of learning, then, in an intellectual, abstractive, reflective, and symbolic conception, nor, by contrast, as a conditioning reaction process, but rather as an "engagement"—as a personal self-commitment. The whole person, in the psychomatic sense of emotions, instincts and soma as well as intellectual and voluntary abilities, is involved in such self-commitment.

We are also contrasting this kind of engaged or self-committed learning with a learning process that is the result of competitive motivation and is often simply defensive learning. We can find a person who learns under the stress of competition and in emotional stress doing

77

well in terms of marks or grades. But in fact, he can later have an extremely negative reaction about what he has learned, so much so that he has developed a hostility about remembering it. This can sometimes actually result in not merely a negative and resistant attitude towards what he had learned and even received a good grade in, but he can be so traumatized by the experience that he remains very hostile to the subject. When this happens he may turn away, in aversion, from the whole area of knowledge that this negative learning experience represents for him.

By contrast we are speaking of learning which is measured finally by the degree to which the person himself has genuinely invested himself and so holds a very positive feeling and identifies his total self with the subject after his learning experience.

By considering this self-investment aspect of a whole person in learning, and not simply what he knows or can give back to the teacher in some intellectual form, we are also bringing closer together the learning and the counseling process. Seen this way, the process by which a person invests himself in what he is learning, and the counseling therapy by which a person invests in what he wants to be and begins to fulfill it, are very similar.

We therefore see that we are no longer separating counseling therapy from learning by seeing counseling in a health or growth model, and the learning process as something different. Rather we are bringing these together and are calling them all learning either at a personal level or at a broader, educational, social, and cultural level.

This idea of course is not new. If we consider the old axiom about "whatever is received is received according to the manner of the one receiving," it becomes quite evident that the whole personality structure of the learner is basic to what he finally learns as a personal self-investment.

What we are proposing is that the degree of student self-investment should be the main focus of learning rather than simply whether adequate knowledge has been presented and intellectually understood and memorized by the student. Basic to the measurement of real learning is not simply what the student gives back in evidence that he knows but what he has personally invested in and is identified with.

This would therefore involve us in fundamental concepts that are not only conscious but unconscious in the student. We would also see emerging in the learning process as in counseling therapy implicit as well as explicit personal value systems which aid or impede the student's cooperation in the learning experience.

Moreover, fundamental aspects in our culture itself—for example, the tendency to depersonalization and abstract problem solving rather than to genuine investment in one another as persons—are often factors in conflict within the student himself as he struggles to invest in the knowledge that he has been receiving.

These conceptions and others that could be added bring the learning process to the intense somatic, instinctive, emotional involvement of the client in counseling therapy. It also reveals that the student's state of self-worth seems to determine the degree to which he can learn in this way, that is, openly and without defense. He sees learning, not as something attacking him and from which he must defend himself with a good, or at least a passing grade, but as something positively invoking his genuine self-investment and permanent self-identification.

To catch this complicated process, therefore, we have called this an incarnate and redemptive as well as a self-investment process of learning. In order for this kind of self-investment in learning to occur, there must often be the kind of acceptance not simply of an intellectual judgmental self but also of an emotional and instinctive self—as part of one's whole self and as having genuine worth. Only after such total incarnate-redemptive self-acceptance can a genuine investment of self take place. This we see as similar to the kind of struggle with conflicting aspects of the self that is often revealed in a process of counseling therapy. We see the same incarnate redemptive process as necessary to self-invested learning.

For this presentation we will draw heavily as a model from linguistic research we have been doing over a period of years.* In this linguistic model, we are not as such focused on or concerned about grammar and vocabulary, but about observing the process by which a person learns to speak a foreign language through and in the presence of natives of that language.

From this point of view we are thinking of learning as a personal relationship similar to counseling therapy. We have used the phrase, "learning is persons," to catch the intense relationship that goes on as people are speaking together in a foreign language. Into this group learning experience, we have tried to incorporate the deep rapport, understanding, and sensitivity that has to exist if the counseling therapy process is to be effective.

Looking at counseling therapy from a learning model, we can propose that on a level of self-knowledge, the knowing teacher is, in fact, the "I." There is a blocking between the "I" and the "myself" when the acting self, the "myself," does not carry out what the "I" proposes. It is this blocking that causes the conflict, confusion, pain

*This has been reported in detail in Charles A. Curran, *Counseling & Psychotherapy: The Pursuit of Values,* New York, 1968, pp. 295–351.

and guilt which the client often expresses at the beginning of counseling therapy with expressions such as "I am really disgusted with myself."

In the educative process a similar blocking often occurs between the teacher and the student who, in his state of confusion and conflict, is unable to learn what the teacher knows and is proposing to him.

Considering therefore a counseling therapy model of learning and learning as persons, we can focus on those things which, in our linguistic research we found basic to the learning process. This learning process was marked by a transition from extreme dependency, anxiety, fear and a kind of primitive, almost embryonic state in the learner to a growing independence. This was finally indicated by an almost dramatic determination on the learner's part to be independent, accompanied by feelings of anger and strong self-assertion. We had therefore a continuum from a highly dependent state extending from Stage I through V where, in Stage V, there was intense self-determination, basic self-esteem and forceful self-assertion against being dependent and so wanting to have learning internalized in the self.

At the first stage (St. Paul's concepts of "milk for babes" and the law as pedagogue can be seen this way), one could think of ignorance as being similar to illness. Both force us into a kind of invalid state of regression where we are fearful, anxious and dependent. Growing health like gaining knowledge is the gradual mobilization of forces within ourselves pushing us back out into independent existence.

The continuum seemed to begin with anxiety and dependency and extend out to aggression and self-determination. The contrasting states of submissive anxiety and confident aggression would be at the extreme ends of the continuum. The process along this continuum

81

was characterized by the growing of something intrinsic to the self. The self in the process will only tolerate the initial states of dependency and anxiety for which a kind of paternal or maternal embryonic support is helpful, until it can gain sufficient knowledge, courage and self-assertion to an independent state. One can expect this independent growth continuum in learning provided nothing is done to impede, interrupt or be in conflict with it.

In this, the teacher could be seen as the midwife in learning, in Plato's sense. The physician is often thought of as someone who has simply learned to do the things that do not impede nature's process of enabling the person to become healthy again. He does not so much heal as remove the impediments to nature's process. Looked at this way, the teacher would be primarily like the physician. He would do only those things which further those internal forces in the person himself that lead towards independent learning.

Stated another way we are talking about the internalization of knowledge in contrast to its initial state of externalization. Simply to assert knowledge from the outside so that it is intellectually understood is, at best, a beginning process that should lead to the real internalization of learning. For this internalization to take place, the self must invest totally. Therefore his anxieties, his fears, his needs for dependency all must be understood and engaged as in the initial stages of counseling. As these forces are assuaged and understood, new forces of self-assertion, anger and desire for independence begin to show themselves. At the final stage it is this independent self-assertion which marks the internalization of knowledge. There is a complete cessation of dependency on the outside knower because now what the knower represents has been internalized and constitutes aspects of a new self for the learner.

We are applying then to learning what a generation ago we began to apply to the relationships of guidance, counseling and therapy, namely, that it is only superficially helpful or may even impede the person, to tell him from the outside what he ought to do.

As counseling skills developed, they focused not on external knowledge but on the internal self-awareness of the client. His struggle with himself to carry out what he was told to do, or what he already knew to do, was far more important than purely extrinsic advice or guidance or "if I were you" type of counseling. This awareness has application to learning in the sense that purely external-ized knowledge is at best only a first stage and is usually already somewhat known by the learner. The core dif-ficulty here is his real internalizing of the matter of learning. To resolve this difficulty engages us in many of the same psychological subtleties that have already been revealed over the last twenty years in our vast research on the personal counseling process.

## Mimetic Internalization

In our linguistic research, the following explanation of the five steps of the learning-counseling relationship was given to each prospective learner:

STAGE I.    The client is completely dependent on the language counselor.

1. First, he expresses *only* to the counselor and *in English,* what he wishes to say to the group. Each group member overhears this English exchange, but is not involved in it.

2. The counselor then reflects these ideas back to the client *in the foreign language* in a warm, accepting tone, in simple language especially of cognates, in phrases of five or six words.

3. The client turns to the group and presents his ideas *in the foreign language!* He has the counselor's aid if he mispronounces or hesitates on a word or phrase.

This is the client's *maximum security stage.*

STAGE II.

1. Same as above (1).

2. The client turns and begins to speak the *foreign language* directly to the group.

3. The counselor aids only as the client hesitates or turns for help. These small independent steps are signs of positive confidence and hope.

STAGE III.

1. The client speaks directly to the group *in the foreign language*. This presumes that the group has now acquired the ability to understand his simple phrases.

2. Same as (3) above. This presumes the client's greater confidence, independence and proportionate insight into the relationship of phrases, grammar and ideas. Translation given only when a group member desires it.

STAGE IV.

1. The client is now speaking freely and complexly *in the foreign language*. Presumes group's understanding.

2. The counselor directly intervenes in grammatical error, mispronunciation or where aid in complex expression is needed. The client is sufficiently secure to take correction.

STAGE V.

1. Same as IV.

2. Counselor intervenes not only to offer correction but to add idioms and more elegant constructions.

3. At this stage, the client can become counselor to group in Stages I, II, and III.

The actual progress towards independent speaking of the foreign language was designed this way:

I. Total dependence on language counselor. Idea said in English, then said to group in foreign language, as counselor slowly and sensitively gives each word to the client.

84

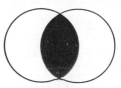

II. Beginning courage to make some attempts to speak in the foreign language as words and phrases are picked up and retained.

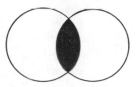

III. Growing independence with mistakes that are immediately corrected by counselor.

IV. Needing counselor now only for idioms and more subtle expressions and grammar.

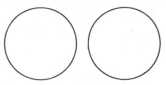

V. Independent and free communication in the foreign language. Counselor's *silent* presence reinforces correctness of grammar and pronunciation.

White=growth towards independent self expression.

After a period in Stage I, each learner gradually began to acquire words, then phrases, which he used independently. By Stage IV, he could speak and be understood on his own, still making mistakes. At this stage, many immigrants, for example, stop improving their English because they can be understood and other people no longer intervene to help them.

Since detailed explanations have been given elsewhere, we will limit here our description of this linguistic self-invested process.

We have called this kind of learning a mimetic internalization process. Learning begins with a mimetic bind between learner and knower (from Plato's ideas of mimesis or representation as fundamental to learning). A learning contract is established—similar to a counseling contract—when a person knows in an organized way what someone wishes to learn. The knower is thus mimetic to or representative of what the learner wishes finally to know and be. This mimetic bind can be indicated by the learner having paid fees and enrolled for a course or even simply by his presence in a class. Much of the conflict and resistance in the initial steps of learning do not therefore indicate unwillingness to learn as is sometimes thought but rather are similar to the conflict and resistance often experienced in the early stages of counseling. They are part of the disorganized psychomatic state of the learner and, rightly understood, evidence of his genuine desire of self-investment. He simply needs help in the learning experience as he does in counseling, in order to make this desire for genuine self-commitment effective.

In our learning research therefore we spoke not of teachers but of learning-counselors. This was to designate the warm, understanding and considerate way the learning counselors accepted the confused and disordered anxious or hostile states of the learners. Thus understood and accepted in their learning and personal conflicts and confusion, the learners, like clients in counseling, began the slow but steady process of learning self-investment and mimetic internalization.

## CONCLUSION

We are proposing then that our present educative process has been primarily intellectual, reflective and abstractive and largely removed from personal engagement. In the use of words that oddly have disappeared in English, "tract" and "flect," we might arrive again at the original conceptions of learning in which we first engage ourselves as persons with one another, "tracting and flecting." After this, then, we can begin to abstract and reflect on these personal experiences.

So, for example, in using our language model, when we dealt with rules of grammar or extension of vocabulary, we did so out of the experiences of the group themselves in which they had deeply invested their feelings, their instinctive defenses, their deep somatic reactions. From this material, recorded and written so that it became a lesson plan, if one were to use that old fashioned term, it was then pointed out that certain consistent rules were being used in these spontaneous expressions. Upon reflection, the group could grow to recognize and gradually internalize vocabulary changes and better adaptation to the rules themselves.

What emerged then was the realization that while life, in terms of a foreign language communication, is spontaneous, free, personal and intense and so is emotional and somatic as well as intellectual and voluntary, it is not without some internal form or order. Upon abstraction and reflection, one grows to see this internal form and order as being basically necessary for adequate communication and understanding. In this sense rules of grammar and vocabulary, while dead structures that need to be brought alive when they have been memorized or learned, were, in these experiences, first contained in their spontaneous expressions. Somewhat as people may be surprised in the study of anatomy to discover that these skeletal structures are contained in the living people that they know and love, so our students were surprised and excited to see that grammar and vocabulary were really alive and basic to the rich, warm communications they were having with one another in the foreign language.

One might conclude then that while no one loves a skeleton, yet skeletons are basic to our whole body structure. In a certain sense one might say that by always proceeding from abstractions, remoteness and non-humanness in human learning, we are in a way, forcing the child or adult to that inhuman experience of finding a skeleton loveable, whereas what he usually finds is either fearful or comic. Perhaps we need to rethink learning in much the same terms.

We are suggesting here, too, that the incarnation-redemption dynamic by which the removed concept of God of the intellectual Greeks became the human God of the Jews, and Christians, might have a further learning dynamic parallel. The removed and almost god-like figure of the teacher might also need to become man and incarnately present himself in a genuine and deep total personal relationship with the learner. Only then perhaps can learning become truly redemptive and convey a new sense of worth and self-esteem on the learner. In this way the teacher must decrease, the learner increase. This process continues until a "new man," in the learning sense, comes into being. This results from the positive self-investment and internalization of knowledge in the learner who then no longer needs the external knower. It is the teacher's great achievement, then, to be no longer needed.

The Church, then, seen in this sense as a knowing-learning community, is invested with an incarnate redemptive intensity that a political model or an abstractive or conditioning model cannot give. It is a redemptive community as each one increases in Christ-like value and meaning and conveys this in his respectful regard both towards himself and others.

# V. The Need for Creative Listeners

IN considering the need for listeners, one can quickly come up with a kind of nightmarish image of a world filled with people speaking furiously over telephones everywhere, into phones that are off the hook with no one listening. Perhaps no need is so dramatically emphasized in all the shouting that is around us as the need for someone to be genuinely, deeply and profoundly committed to listening to what is being said. It is listening that is the redemptive act. It is the Logos, the Second Person, the perfect understander that is at the same time the Redeemer out of whose relationship with the Father is generated perfect love. It is this kind of concept of the need for redemptive listening that we mean here. Redemptive listening means the deep convalidation that comes to me when someone genuinely hears what I say and deeply and sensitively understands it. This is someone of whom afterwards, in the glow of worth that I feel about myself as a result of that experience, I can say with depth of meaning, "He truly understood me; he is a deeply understanding man." By such a word, "understanding," I bring forth, in its resonances, to every hearer an experience of the most profound sort, an experience of compassion and *misericordia* in this kind of delicate and sensitive listening that heals wounds and cures and which redeems with the sense of worth and value that it conveys to the

90

person. It is in this sense then that we are going to focus on the need for listeners.

The title "The Need For Creative Listeners" might be extended to mean something of what, in the biblical sense, Solomon prayed for and received, namely, the understanding heart; or in the Hebrew, a listening heart. We might also make this title more formal, in the literal sense of the word "formal," by speaking of the art and skill of creative listening. We could even extend this further by talking about incarnate-redemptive listening or communication. Both these extensions could be considered facets of the title, "The Need For Creative Listeners."

## CREATIVE INCARNATE COMMUNICATION

The kind of listening, or creative communication, which is both incarnate and redemptive, leaves both the communicator and communicant filled with worth and positive motivation because it takes in the whole person as a communication—not merely an intellectualized segment of the person. This kind of communication does not come about naturally; it is an acquired, defined, concentrated, conscious and directed effort that skillfully engenders the communication process which is the end product of the art and skill of listening.

It is this kind of listening which is creative. It incarnates *both* persons and thereby renders them whole in their communication with one another. It also leaves them filled with a deep sense of convalidating worth. This is, then, a convalidating communication or a communicative convalidation. It is the kind of relationship which, between two or more people, is redemptive because it leaves each one enhanced in regard to their own significance and meaning in the Christian sense of having experienced what it means to be bought at a great price. It does this not only

91

for the person himself, but also it enhances him in the appreciation of, and regard for, the validity and depth and meaning of his own ideas. These ideas were worthy of communication and they brought about a personal redemption when the person struggled to communicate them.

In speaking of the art and skill in creative communication, the person communicating his ideas becomes aware of the value of himself and of what he is trying to say because of the art and skill of the receiver and his response. What is being emphasized here is that redemptive communication as an art and skill is not something that just happens naturally but requires a conscious effort on the part of the listener to make it possible. The focal point here, then, is the nature of this ability to produce an incarnate-redemptive communication which is convalidating for both the person himself and his ideas.

## PROTECTIVE COMMUNICATION

There is an art and skill involved in redemptive communication. Whenever two people communicate together, whether in counseling or in a more superficial exchange, one of the main primitive motives that influences them, and therefore influences the communication, is a simple basic defense of the self. The result is that just the effort itself to communicate is very threatening so that in the very effort to communicate the person is simultaneously protecting himself from getting through to the other. In this contradictory position the person is defeated in his attempt to communicate. It is because of the fear of being hurt, because of some vague catastrophic anxiety, that it is necessary consciously to acquire an art and skill in both communication itself and listening. Otherwise the fear is enhanced and heightened not only on the part of the receiver. And of course, the fear, both on the part of the communicator and on the part of the receiver, may well be justified since both, in fact, have been hurt in the past.

What we see here then is a double art and skill: the receptive person, the listener, must dovetail into and facilitate the art and skill of the communicator that the communicator may be able to overcome his defenses and protective linguistics, and consequently, genuinely trust himself to be open to the receiver.

This is communication viewed as an art that needs to be learned. But in the effort to practice this art, one is the victim of his own fear of the other's rejection, and so he fails to communicate at all. In calling it an art and skill that has to be acquired, we mean that one person has to learn to be open, to trust the other person. There is a dual kind of skill both in being able to be receptive to another and also helping the other to be open. One of the reasons this does not come naturally is that its natural expression is inhibited by the fear the communicator has that he will be rejected.

## The Redemptive Listener

The question to be raised now is which art comes first, that of communicating or that of receiving. The answer to this is expressed in the title. The atmosphere, the matrix of the setting into which the communicator is about to project himself, must first reveal itself to him as non-threatening, as something in which he might at least be encouraged to risk communicating. To provide this atmosphere, the listener must communicate first his real listening capacity, since the communicator has a need for a listener, but he also needs some assurance that here is a true listener, a true understanding heart. It is into this true listener that he can take the risk of openly plunging himself in his communication, rather than turning aside in a protective, conflicting, and self-defeating way. Without the true listener, his communication will result in self-protection rather than an open commitment. There must be something in the listener's manner, and something in what he has first communicated that defines him as an understanding heart. It is only in this atmosphere that the communicator's need for a listener can be fulfilled.

Communication will not take place then unless and until the receiver shows that he is a person who can be trusted. Where non-convalidating communication exists, in the sense of ordinary communication, this atmosphere of trust must first be established by the receiver before redemptive communication can take place. It is paradoxical, but the only milieu in which the communicator can open himself up is one in which he feels the person is really receiving him, and then he is able to put aside his blocking and defenses and truly exercise his art of communication. In other words, he must feel a reciprocal milieu before he is able to do this.

It is important that the listener not only feel receptive but he must show this in some manner to the communicator. It is his, the receiver's gift of himself, that comes first. In this sense, it is the listener who loves first, in assuring the communicator that his need for a listener will be realized.

We have used the expression "incarnate-redemptive" communication, and both of these words are important. One might say, in using the word "redemptive," that whatever else the listener may communicate of himself, essentially what he must communicate is a redemptive atmosphere. By this is meant that he creates a quality and tone that allows the one in need of him, the communicator, to believe and trust and therefore begin to open up.

94

So whatever he says, and in whatever manner he says it, as a result, the communicator will feel himself a worthy person in the receiver's mind, and therefore is redeemed. Consequently, the communicator is assured in advance that whatever he says will be genuinely appreciated and worthily understood—it will not be distorted or misinterpreted or mishandled. One of the great impediments that prevents the communicator from openness is his fear that what he says will be segmented, distorted, twisted, and not really redemptively received. And when what he says is not received in its true worth, he himself will be rejected as not *being* of any true worth.

The listener has to communicate the idea that he will accept the communicator and not distort him; that he will accept him for his true worth and give him his due value; that no matter what he says, this acceptance of him will continue. This atmosphere will give the communicator the assurance that he can take the risk of making a mistake in what he communicates and still be accepted. This is a redemptive atmosphere or a redemptive aura in which the acceptance of the listener is radiated back to the communicator. Thus, there quickly enters into the communication this redemptive atmosphere that allows the communicator to take the risk. The receiver then takes an active role in creating an atmosphere in which the giver is free to let down his defenses.

## NON-INVESTED COMMUNICATION

The word "incarnate" is extremely important here also, because one of the most basic defenses that a person has is that of reducing communication to an abstractive intellectualizing. This does not really involve the person in any communication. Although he may give the appearance of communicating himself, in fact, he never really communi-

95

cates himself at all. This type of intellectualizing is protective of the person because if what is said is misunderstood or distorted or twisted, he can rationalize out of it on the basis that he was not involved in the first place. He does not need to defend a position since he never really took one. All he did was make a series of abstracted intellectualizations; there was no incorporation, no incarnation, no deep self-investment in what he said. Consequently, the person's intellectualized statements afford him a maximum amount of protection. The most basic threat then to genuine communication is the subtlety with which the person can rationalize his suppressed anxieties about not being heard or validated or redeemed in a communication. He does this by intellectualizing, since this precludes self-investment.

Alternately, the person might speak in such a way that no one could include him in the investment of what he has said; for example, he might talk about things, or other people, or various kinds of facts that are neutral or scientific. But this in no way engages the person in self-commitment; a person may communicate generally in that way or teach in such a manner. In the incarnate sense, then, one of the defenses that can be assumed is that the speaker may go off into intellectualizing and factual information. In doing this, he does not invest himself, so that if what he says is not understood, he can simply say that he was talking about generalities or facts. But this is a way of keeping himself from becoming incarnate.

An illustration of this would be that non-self-invested teaching in which the teacher stays in abstractions and principles, or removed conceptions. Or conversely, one becomes very scientific, but scientific in the neutral, one-way-glass-mirror sense. Both of these kinds of masked communication are merely disguises for a communication that allows no openness into which the students can make an investment, since there was nothing really there in which to invest. They either understand or they do not, and the teacher grades them accordingly, but there is no risk or commitment involved on either side.

The difficulty with this is that the students will not likely really learn anything personally significant because they are not given anything redemptive in which to invest themselves. This seems to be one of the issues now being raised on university campuses, namely, that this protective kind of communication, appearing under the guise of intellectualized abstraction or scientific factual demonstrations, has totally depersonalized the student. The student feels this depersonalization confusedly without knowing exactly why. He is simply left with the feeling of not being able to commit himself personally; the communication itself does not allow it.

This depersonalization occurs because the teacher wants to protect his feelings from being hurt if he were to risk going out and reaching the student. This is the risk in becoming incarnate. Without this risk, the student never feels anything human; what he feels is impersonal scientific data or abstracted concepts being thrown out at him. The teacher who feels such a need for defense might be thought to remain in the protective embryonic or pre-natal stage of personal commitment. He is afraid to be born into a genuine relationship with others because this would mean that he has to be seen as a human being. The communication is cut off on both sides: on the part of the teacher, in his refusing to become incarnate; and on the part of the student, in his lack of opportunity to invest in anything personal.

## THE NATURE
## OF INCARNATE-REDEMPTIVE COMMUNICATION

But whether we speak of teaching and learning or of even more deeply psychological encounters, the quality of the communications would be creative, would be incarnately redemptive, would be open, only if they would center on a listening heart in the emotional, instinctive, and somatic sense of heart. If the communication is to be a communication of the whole self of the person who needs to be listened to, a great part of his need will be fulfilled if he is secure enough and free enough that he can begin to trust. But to do this, trust must be conveyed to him first. He can then begin to trust not only his own ideas and his intellectualizing processes but his spontaneity as well. For his spontaneity to be trusted, he must allow his feelings to come through, he must let those ideas in which he is really invested show their self-investment by his own incarnate expression. He must get excited and be allowed to; he must be free to be angry, and be allowed to; he must be free to let himself be depressed or frustrated or confused or elated or enthusiastic. All these concepts of negative and positive feeling-incarnation must be allowed. He must also be sufficiently trustful of the redemptive quality of the listeners that his primitive instinct for self-defense is unhooked and he can let himself flow into the communication with some reassurance that he will not be destroyed.

## THE EXPRESSION OF IDEAS THROUGH AFFECT

In a word, the freedom that an incarnate-redemptive atmosphere would produce would allow the communicator to communicate himself spontaneously and without defense, in *affective* language. He would be able to let his affects flow in and through the ideas that they are invested in. With this flow of both affect and ideas, what is of really deep value to him as a self will be contained in this expression. Unless real personal values are hidden here, he would not have such deep feelings and the idea would not encapsulate him with its affective quality. Out of the spontaneous expression and then examination of such affectively packaged ideas will come an awareness of basic values which he can begin to disentangle and distinguish and so see their significance to himself. We are talking not only about affects, then, but about affects as they are communicated in and through spontaneous communication that contains ideas and personal self-investments as well.

It is relatively easy to communicate ideas alone, but in order for a person to communicate affects as well, he has to have some assurance that not only will his ideas be received but that his feelings also will be received. In this way he will be able to express together his ideas, his affects and his values.

In order then for the creative self to come out, the affective self must be released. The person has to trust that his ideas will come through in his spontaneity. Within this is encapsulated his own self-investment, which at some point will reveal hidden values, but which are known only through his affect around these ideas. He cannot know himself in purely intellectualized versions of himself. This would only make him an oral character in the traditional protective sense, and this never leads to self-knowledge, but rather to self-disguise.

In a sense a person does not become himself until he is free to express his feelings and they are accepted. Since the affects would not be present unless he were invested in the ideas they contain, by protecting himself from express-

99

ing feelings, he is protecting his personal ideas. This is why such ideas will not be communicated until he is free to communicate the affects around them. He will never then clearly see the ideas that he is invested in because he is too afraid to let his emotions spontaneously come.

## CREATIVE SPONTANEITY

The surrealists understood well the protective device of intellectualization or rationalization or appearing to be logical or formal in the traditional poetic form. They rejected this because they felt no real communication occurred. However, they were misled in their understanding of form; what they were groping for was the notion that by genuine spontaneity one would reach authentic self-invested ideas or, in other words, one would reach the truth of oneself, which would be indicative of a true communication.

What the surrealists saw was that logic and form were not reaching the human person, and so they rejected them in an attempt to reach man through his spontaneous affects. Because logic and form and intellectualization could not reach man, they swung to the opposite extreme and placed all the emphasis on feelings. What they were groping for, however, was the realization that from a feeling will come one's personal values hidden like gems in the center. Somewhere in the unfathomed depths of the self, a real self-knowledge may be found. The process of creativity then is the process of discovery. Surrealist spontaneity alone however will not bring about this creativity because it does not go beyond itself. Rather, the spontaneity has to be distilled in order to get at the true communication of self that it contains.

Another aspect of spontaneous communication which can be personally helpful, but which will not lead to the integrated self-awareness that we are talking about here, is the concept of ventilation. The encountering of a warm listener who entices me to let my affects flow, and in that way to ventilate my emotional self, is assuredly helpful. It allows a catharsis and a release of the self which other structures may not permit. But the difficulty with ventilation is that, somewhat like a filling-station conception, one needs to do it repeatedly; that is, it seems not to do anything about the situation in a fundamental way. While it is relieving, it is so only in releasing something which will pile up again. Thus ventilation alone, any more than surrealist spontaneity, both of which have some worth, does not lead finally to this inner self-integrative communication and knowledge.

The surrealist emphasis on acceptance of emotionality alone was not enough, then, nor is simply a conception of ventilation; both lack form. The listener does not really help someone find himself by letting him ventilate only. Rather it takes some kind of creative listening—listening that has cognitive form as well as affect—to help a person distill his real self from his affects. Ventilation is a one-way communication in that the person empties himself of a superficial self but does not fill himself with a real self. He simply ventilates the covering; he never uncovers the real self—he never *discovers.*

## DISCOVERY OF THE SELF

One of the important things we have learned from research in counseling and psychotherapy especially, but also from the other communication arts, is an awareness of a double-language communication. The listener needs to acquire a profound and perceptive ability to understand the implications, both affective and cognitive, of a person's communication. Both affects—somatic, instinctive,

101

and emotional, and cognition-inner awareness of others and the self—form an important part of any communication that is spontaneous and free on the part of the secure and trusting communicator. This demands a highly sensitive ear that grasps what the affects are that are being communicated and feels with them in the deepest sense of the Greek *sympatheia,* sympathy. At the same time this understanding penetrates into the self-investments which these spontaneous emotions encapsulate—penetrates them and therefore grasps what they genuinely contain.

The speaker must feel free then to make a total communication of himself in order that he may become aware of what he says and is, or in other words, to find that gem of himself hidden in his affect, in his emotional self. In seeing the "gem" he will see the total relationship and the gem all at one time. If he is angry and free to communicate it, the listener hears not only his anger, but, gradually, what is behind *why* he is angry, and he helps him to explore this. That is to say, the listener reaches in his cognitive understanding into the hypothalamic expression that comes up through the whole neurological system. This would be the instinctive, somatic, affective and emotional world of communication that the person has struggled in some cortical way to put into words. It is through those confused words that the listener senses his whole affective world. When the speaker then hears this expressed back to him, it fits his hypothalamic inner world and he feels the resulting relief. It is this core relief that gives the speaker the deep feelings of being understood. He usually expresses this relief by nodding, by a sigh, often by "That's it!", or "Yes, that's just the way I feel!" or "That's exactly it—that really fits!"

Such expressions convey almost an organismic relief. Because the response fits so well, the person feels his whole self validated. When the person hears that his affects are understood at a cognitive level, he finds himself raised up to that cognitive level, and can then continue, step by step, to discover himself.

The speaker needs an understanding of his language of affect from the listener. The listener then must be a linguist in affective communication if he is to reach the subtle meanings of the speaker. But simply to presume that the language of affect is the only language he needs would be misleading. It is this simplification which leads to a confusion between ventilation and constructive communication. If the only language that the listener has is the understanding of affect, he will largely resonate merely with his own affects at a greater or lesser level. He will have shared in some measure the same type of affect and he will say so or show so in his manner. But he then becomes a reverberating or resonant affective object like the string of a violin. This however will be no more than a resonating response that encourages ventilation but adds nothing further.

One must respond not just to the language of affect, but he must also be aware of other kinds of personal language as well and be able to respond to these. Speaking only affective language will allow continued ventilation but it will not reach the core being of the person.

## INCARNATIONAL AND REDEMPTIVE COGNITION

This leads to another side of human communication—the cognitive intellectual side. If this is misstated, that is, if it is taken out of its incarnational quality, it will be what we seemed to reject, namely, an intellectual formalism. But what will save us from that view is the notion of an incarnational cognition and its corollary, incarnational and redemptive symbolization. This is not simply an intellec-

103

tualization that is reflective and abstractive, but a process that is truly concerned with "flecting and tracting." By this we mean that such a cognitive process is incorporated in the actual experience of the whole invested self. The words "cognitive" *and* "symbolic" then are meant here in an incarnate, redemptive sense and not in the formalized, abstractive, defensive, protective, and intellectualizing implication that we rejected originally.

This incarnational cognitive process can lead to the discovery of self-values because by definition the person had to be invested in an experience for it to become hypothalamic and affective. It is not just cold intellectualism. It has to have an affective quality to it. While language of affect alone is not enough, and while the abstract intellectualization is not enough either, the notion of an incarnational reflective intellectualization catches the idea of an inner value pursuit. But to arrive here, we must be considering "flecting" as well as reflecting. The awareness must be drawn out of the suffering, the elation and the self-investment of the hypothalamic communication itself. We are talking then about reflecting on "flecting." It is necessary to abstract what one has been actually "tracting" and to reflect on what has also been genuinely "flecting" and not simply to intellectualize.

## THE NEED FOR SYMBOLIZATION

What is unique to man is that he needs to be symbolized in order to be free to understand himself. A symbol is a way of freeing one from the confines of one's unique individuation. One is unfree so long as he is bound to his unique self. One's affective bind has a person uniquely individualized in his communication. But when the understanding listener grasps the nature of the other person's affective

104

communication, he responds not simply at the level of the uniqueness of his bind that he too has shared—thus resulting in two unique binds—but he responds with sensitively tuned cognition that adequately symbolizes the feelings in which the person is isolated. This allows him to go beyond himself: it frees the person to move out of himself. He can then begin to know, study, and reflect upon those aspects that are encapsulated in the unique, highly individualized emotional-instinctive-somatic components that were contained in his affective language.

One might say then that the really creative listener who is incarnately redemptive of the other first of all frees him by responding, not in the language of affect, but in the language of cognition. Such a response tries to give some kind of adequate self-symbols that the person can hold on to and which then enable him not simply to feel about himself but to begin to know about himself. This would lead not simply to *sympatheia* but to *gnosis,* to profound personal awareness.

The listener, by symbolizing the feelings of the other, frees him from his alienation and allows him a feeling of generic belonging. He is one with the human race when he is adequately symbolized, whereas when he is involved simply in his affect, he is all alone. His adequate cognitive symbolization de-alienates him. It makes him human rather than alone in his unique feeling world.

## REDEMPTIVE SYMBOLIZATION

The listener who can do this sets up a communication and a community through which the person is taken out of himself. The heart of the redemptive element in this is that it frees one from his ''damned'' aloneness and

105

redeems him into belonging, into a state where he can begin to feel and understand that his uniqueness is now shared.

This redemptive quality of the listener's responses takes the person out of the loneliness, alienation, and confusion of his feeling world and leads him to an understanding of the nature of his feelings through a more adequate symbolization of them. But the responses go further. They also penetrate the nature of what it is the person is really seeking, wants and cares about which lies behind his feelings. These are the goals, the purposes, the persons and the situations which he may not have clearly seen before but which are implicit in his feeling world—even when only the feelings are consciously known. This process leads the person to say, sometimes with surprise, "Yes, that is what I want; that is the reason why I was so depressed and that is why now I have been so delighted."

In other words the person might feel anger, depression, or joy and yet not explicitly recognize the cause. Its adequate symbolization on the part of the skilled cognitive listener who is understanding his language of affect leads him to the "why" of his feelings. The most widely used word among small children is this word "why." Spontaneously behind any affect is the need for this inquiring cognition. It is this need that the cognitive-affective understanding listener supplies in his responses, as well as the need for the person to have his affects understood. He supplies the person's need to know why—why he is so affective around this person, place or thing. This leads to personal values—to goals and purposes one has already invested in, even though unconsciously.

Affective communication is both verbal and somatic. The listener must take this into consideration and distill from it the cognitions that are there and give them back to the speaker. By such an affective-cognitive process the listener conveys the feeling that he has received the affect, but in symbolization he is also giving back to the person the "why." In ordinary relationships we are often woefully inadequate in regard to ourselves and others because either we simply see ourselves as abstractive people, using abstraction as a protection from communication, or alternately we see ourselves and others just as feeling people and get caught up in our own uniqueness of feelings. But we are really "feeling-why" people. In the feeling is the "why." The adequate affective-cognitive listener reaches not only the affects, with all the hypothalamic reverberations that they contain, but he leads us to the "why" of these affects, the "why" being the measure of one's self-engagement to a goal, a person, a situation or a series of personal values behind them. This allows a person not only to see them, but having seen them, it can help him "re-sort" them, discharging and disengaging himself from some, holding on even more preciously to others and acquiring new ones. All affects then are both goal-directed and self-invested in some measure or they would not be affects.

The communication comes from the lips of the speaker to the ear of the listener. The latter symbolizes and returns it to the speaker who is himself in need of this communication, both on the cortical level and also in a way that satisfies the hypothalamus—the brain center of feelings and instincts—because it "fits." This is a moment of high humanity because it is no longer just a redemptive ventilation of feelings; it is a communication of feelings at the very highest level of the person's self-understanding, which is integratively redeeming. While the speaker communicated as a segmented isolated person, he hears himself back as an integrated whole. This is the heart of the redemptive aspect of his incarnate communication, namely that he has been made whole in the most profound sense of the derivative health and of the corresponding *salus*.

The only way that a person can become whole—that he can "pull himself together"—is to first go outside of himself and then come back in. While the element of validation through the other is contained in the other's very listening presence, more than this is necessary. It is a truly delicate skill that enables one person to be genuinely redemptive of the other through what he says. But if what the listener says does not fit the hypothalamus of the speaker, if it does not reach the affects, it is merely abstract, depersonalized and offensive, even though it be true.

## UNCREATIVE LISTENING

The art and skill of listening is in a very special way in demand because in addition to the impediments of threat and anxiety that the person needing to be heard has in his own openness, there is on the other side an extremely aggressive need on the part of the other person, not really to listen, but to be listened to. Although there is everywhere a vast number of people who need listeners, there are very few who will discipline themselves to the art and skill of listening.

One might even magnify this by proposing that there is all sorts of shouting but nobody listening to any of the shouts. This could be a room filled with shouters or even a court or open public area. The audience is not really an "audience" in the sense of listeners. They are either internally arguing with the speaker, whom they are hearing externally and not really trying to hear what he says, or openly resisting him by opposing him or subtly distorting

108

and blocking the flow of what he is trying to say, by devisive and misunderstanding types of questions upon questions and argument upon argument. These of course lead to confusion and distortion and not to a furthering of the speaker's ideas. Algebraically designed, one might propose that the speaker intended to speak from point one to point five, but never gets to point two, not to mention three, four or five, because the questioner opposes number one by proposing a minus one, and so forces the speaker into minusing, or answering with another minus. The questioner then minuses that equation of minus minus one, etc., with the result that point two is not yet reached. At the end of his alloted time the speaker usually crowds in point three, four, and five in a hurried way. This leaves him and most of his hearers frustrated and disappointed, or angry, or depressed.

This results in a deep sense of not being understood, and the hurt felt after this humiliating experience leaves the speaker or the teacher reluctant to risk himself openly again. He is hurt by such misunderstanding in proportion as he genuinely and creatively tried to invest himself in what he said. The end product is that often what appears to be speaking or lecturing or teaching is, in fact, a form of intellectualized abstraction which is protective of the speaker's self. He is never truly open because he is too afraid of the cruelty he will meet when he tries to be genuinely open. He therefore goes through the appearance of an open presentation but in no way is he self-invested.

The end effect is a depersonalized and aggressive power-control which protects against any real inner relationship with others, under the guise of teaching, a counterpart to the experience of an audience going through the appearance of a communication with no genuine listening. Here we are at the heart of our topic—the need for creative listeners.

## THE RISK OF COMMUNICATION

Experienced circus people say that the one act that all circus people themselves watch and have a never tiring, ever fascinated interest in, is the trapeze act. Now one might consider that the reason that act would never be tiring is because it so profoundly corresponds to the kind of openness present in any truly creative communication. A person takes the risk of letting himself go. He is suspended in air; he can always fall no matter how many times the act was performed before. There is no instance, even if they have done the act one hundred thousand times, wherein one of them cannot fall and badly hurt himself. He must trust the other person to catch him. It could be that right here is the reason why it is so fascinating for even the most experienced of circus workers. Each time a person truly lets himself go he can fall and be gravely hurt. Even the practices require the same skilled degree of art and concentration because every practice is very real. It is somewhere here that we are not only talking about the need for listeners, but in addition the art and skill of the one who listens. Not only is the jump and the letting go necessary if one is to come to live in and through others, but there is also needed the concentrated skill of the one who catches.

When we speak of the need for listeners we speak of two categories of people: one which is in need of being listened to and the other which constitutes the listeners. In this sense the counseling or psychotherapeutic analogy can be misleading, implying as it does that the same person always acts as counselor or therapist, and that a different person acts as the one who is in need of counseling or therapy. But in creative relationships these change. There is a rhythm that people have towards one another, almost like the diastolic and systolic action of the heart, or like breathing. This is the rhythm of life.

Thus at a certain point the one person needs to be listened to, but at another time the other may equally need to be listened to with the same deep understanding. There are no fixed categories here but a kind of breathing rhythm when, at the right moment the listener knows that he is the listener and the speaker knows that he will be delicately, sensitively and artistically listened to. Creative relationships imply a rhythm between people rather than the fixed dichotomized categories of counselor and client, or patient and therapist. It is, as we said earlier, an "M" and "F" interchange.

## THE HUMAN CONDITION

The issue may be raised as to why this redemptive communication would not occur spontaneously—why would we need an art and skill to bring this about? Would it not seem the most natural thing in the world for one person simply to communicate to another at the deepest level of the self? Why should one person be afraid of another? Indeed, why should not the one person wish to get out of his alienation? It is obvious that one does not mistrust others by going around with his eyes closed even though he may be exposed to many unsightly views and even may be hurt seriously sometime. Why cannot the person keep his trust open in the same spontaneous way he keeps his eyes open?

There have been many traditional explanations, basically theological, offered for this. Perhaps no other explanation of original sin is as compelling as that in the beginning it was natural for one to be open, but something in a primeval sense happened to the human race and injected some kind of mistrust into our being. This could be considered as some primal sin that we are born with, which leaves us in an anxiety-ridden and untrusting relationship with others.

Our mistrust and lack of openness to communication might be said then to be the result of some original sin. For many centuries some sort of primal sin had been presupposed: it was tenable since it has always been one of the deepest and most convincing of human experiences. And it is still so convincing today that sophisticated people can believe this.

## A WORLD OF LIARS

This idea has been carried further and if we were to give a title to this special phase of our discussion, it might be called "Satanism Revisited," or even "Satanism Internalized." Another way of dealing with one's fear of being open, one's need to protect himself and one's need to disguise oneself is to say that he is the victim of and strongly under the control of the one who has been called "The Prince of This World" and "The Father of Lies." The Prince of this World, in other words, is a liar. Consequently, there are primal forces against one's being open and trustful, genuine and outgoing. There is a real logic in one's being very careful of what he says and to whom he says it, because these liars will pounce on him and smother him and, in so doing, they will destroy whatever was worthwhile.

The great value of satanism is that it has left the human race with some dignity: it is not exactly vicious people who do this to other persons. There is a prior force, a force of principalities and powers, a satanic force beyond human awareness that works towards this evil and, consequently, Satan is present everywhere. So every time one attempts to communicate oneself, he meets first of all the effects of satanism in what other people do to him.

In answer to the question, "How do you know the presence of Satan in a situation?", traditional spiritual writing has given an interesting description of the actual human situation. They pointed out that Satan is present when one person or a group of people meet marked and unreasonable resistance in striving for an obviously good work, for something that is obviously fine. They explained that this potential good engenders in Satan a resistance and envy so that, in proportion as he sees a good work emerging and realizes the extent and dimension of this work he mounts against it forces of evil, and ensnares as many people as he can within these forces. What this good work will then immediately face, as soon as it attempts to communicate itself, is derision, distortion, segmentation, and misconstruction. Satan's whole effort, so they explain, is to discourage the person who represents this good work, to cause him to give up, to lose courage and not try any more; thus Satan has succeeded.

In this view then we have something that is not internal to the human race but comes to it from the outside. There is a kindness apparent in this viewpoint. In my hurt, for example, I can still feel that it was not your evil, not something that you destructively and viciously did to me; it is just that Satan tempted you and you became his creature in that process. Thus according to one view, the reason we have this mistrust in ourselves is that we were born with the imperfection of original sin. This not only explains our mistrust, it also prevents us from getting out of the suffering of our alienation, and impedes us from knowing where our true selves could have been before we were afflicted with this sin. It is popularly expressed in such sayings as "get the devil out of here,"

113

so that we can communicate without the devil; or "Let's beat the devil out of him." These statements indicate a basic desire to communicate without interference, misunderstanding, and distortion.

## PSYCHOLOGICAL CORRESPONDENCE

Drawing from psychological developments of the past fifty years there is, however, another way of explaining this human situation which corresponds to the shrewd observations of these spiritual writers of an older age. For the situation that they described was one that is very real and endlessly encountered. But we can leave the satanic aspect out of it and look at the psychological factors involved.

The spiritual writers were speaking of an experience we know to be true. This is an experience in which, whenever forces arise that seem to have worth and significance, one is first of all in a deep struggle with himself to have the confidence to dare trust to communicate them. And secondly, when he does dare, having struggled with himself to arrive at the courage to do so, the probabilities are that he will encounter only rarely any kind of creative, constructive response; rather the probabilities are in favor of his encountering a discouraging, depressing response. Many creative people, for example, never speak to anyone about what they are doing until it is formed and viable in the sense of a fetus after seven or eight months, and so their project cannot then be easily hurt by the response they might receive.

Modern psychological writers, beginning with Freud, have treated somewhat differently this same state of distrust and fear of others: man's primal condition. They have "de-Satanized" it and internalized it. In *Beyond the Pleasure Principle,* Freud deals with this under the aspect of death and life. He suggests that inside of each person is a force for death, almost as powerful as any force towards life: a strong death instinct. And he reasons that rather than the simple notion that it ought to be easy for us to open ourselves to life and trust one another, nature has a different intent: everything born has as its goal to die. Consequently, nature has already provided inside the self of each man an instinct which, at the moment one is born, begins to prepare him to die. The moment one begins to live he also begins to die. His goal is death. His purpose is death. His end is death. The whole nature of the organism is to die. And so, buried inside of everything else that the person is, is a powerful instinct to die, to wish death. This is the Freudian death-wish.

Man's inability to be open to communicate can be described in terms of such a death-wish. One has to struggle within himself to bring out anything alive, because to bring anything out of himself that is true, meaningful or valuable is to strive against one's own death-wish. Strong forces in him are aimed at keeping him dead, for then he will be closer to his goal. That is, any life force within him is, in a certain sense, against his nature because it is against what he is born for, which is to die. It is only with great effort that a person struggles to make the first trust to express himself positively. Nor is it natural for the other to respond creatively; he too is born to death. Hence the person's success in bringing something to life and communicating it, only arouses the forces of death in the other. All his death instinct is lined up against the person who has succeeded in presenting something constructive and positive.

## DEATH-WISH DECEPTIVENESS

This death-wish viewpoint can help us look at a common type of intellectual process that often results in self-

115

defeating learning relationships. Early in the counseling therapeutic experience we grew to see that the counselor or therapist had to be completely open to the client, and that he had to accept the client at whatever level of personal expression the client wished to communicate himself. What we learned was that the best way to form a genuine relationship with another person is to avoid approaching him with the preconceived intellectual ideas of what he ought to be, how he ought to express himself, or what he ought to say he intended to do. These attitudes can distort a communication and prevent a genuine relationship. Such preconceptions most often seemed to produce either non-cooperation, or a submissive passivity which, by appearing to do what the therapist or counselor told the person to do, simply masked a supine dependency that was really a negative, passive resistance. We learned that the best approach to a genuine relationship was rather an open committing of oneself to whatever it was that he chose to communicate, and then making an effort to cognize and understand this communication.

This death-wish deception applies with particular force in any learning situation. The teacher in our viewpoint should be seen as client (Stage IV, where the learner helps and understands the knower), not as counselor. It is the student who must act as counselor and who should understand the teacher if learning is to take place. The teacher, like the client, is in deep need of being understood, and to be received and accepted by the student at the intellectual or emotional level of his struggle for creative communication. Reversely, the student is not, in this conception, in the client-patient role but rather in the counselor-therapist role. The teacher who is creative is suffering with ideas that are welled up within him and that he needs to express and have understood. It is the student who can be in the therapeutic position of understanding and genuinely relating to the teacher as he unfolds, often with painful intensity, the ideas that he is invested in.

Seen in this way we have a situation similar to what we have seen in counseling and psychotherapy. By intellectual arguing, the student will not understand the teacher or anything that the teacher has really invested in. On the contrary this type of intellectual argument runs the danger of a death-wish, self-defeating system. It appears to have an intellectual component that is constructive and positive. But this is deceptive. The student, hit with the first excitement of sharing the teacher's self-invested ideas, spontaneously reacts by questioning. The danger is that the student's spontaneous reaction, under the guise of intellectual questioning. arguing or some similar intellectual process, will actually impede his impulse to learn because he has not yet really understood. As a result the teacher's spontaneous freedom to communicate at the deep level of his own creative experience is blocked and frustrated by this initial misunderstanding. Before he is argued with or questioned, the teacher needs, like the client, to be genuinely responded to, accepted and understood.

Consequently we see applied to the learning situation the same subtlety that we have learned from counseling and psychotherapy. It is the teacher who is in need of a genuinely affective-cognitive listener. The student's art and skill of affective-cognitive listening will heighten the learning experience for himself and heighten the creative expression of the teacher.

Similarly in counseling and psychotherapy, insofar as learning is occurring, it is the therapist and counselor who are learning about the client from himself, from the deep painful process of his exploring his own creative self-world. The client himself begins to learn all sorts of depths and dimensions of his own self that he did not know in his

117

initial attempt to express himself and to be understood.

Applied to learning it is the creative teacher who is suffering and in need of being understood. The sensitive understanding art of the student makes him a skilled learner. Once this deep affective-cognitive understanding has occurred between the teacher client and the student learner, we can make way for a second exchange. Here, having grasped what the teacher has creatively invested himself in and has been struggling to communicate, his student-learner may then make his own reverse investment in what he has learned. He is then understood by the teacher in his own creative reaction, and understood also by the other students.

In this we see a creative dynamic, flowing first through the understanding of the student-listener to the creative teacher who needs to be understood. This process must be fulfilled to the complete satisfaction of the teacher's need to be listened to and affectively and cognitively responded to. Then the learners themselves become clients. As a result of the creative process that has been engendered in them, they now need the listening attention and accepting responses of the other learners and of the teacher.

This recalls an observation, representing a long tradition, that one should never argue with another person until one has thoroughly understood him and his ideas. Only when the other person totally accepts our presentation of his ideas are we in a position to argue and disagree. This kind of traditional observation is similar to the creative learning relationship we are describing.

## CONTROLLING THE DEATH-WISH

Where the death-wish defeats the learner is in that situation which occurs in his first impulses to learn, wherein all his life forces are brought forward by the excitement of a new idea. But at the same time all his death-wishes are impelled with equal or greater strength. If he gives in to his first spontaneous urge, it tends not to be really constructive, but impeding. Under the appearance of intellectualizing he actually presents a series of negative arguments and resistances which really reject what the teacher has painfully struggled to present. This rejects and frustrates rather than helps.

In the situation where the student controls his death-wish urge to argue and intellectualize, and actually submits himself to the learning experience, he strives to understand as the counselor tries to understand the client. What occurs here is not intellectual argument, but the flowering, in the learner, of the seeds of what he has received from the creative teacher. It is a flowering of a new self in himself. This is not expressed in intellectual argument or resistance, but on the contrary it comes out with the same need to be understood and listened to and with the same intense, creative excitement as was originally expressed by the creative teacher. Consequently, at this stage, it is the student himself who becomes the teacher of his own creative ideas. These are engendered in him, not in an intellectualized, argumentative process, but in a deeply painful struggle with the new awarenesses that are being born in him as a result of the previous learning insemination.

A familiar illustration of death-life impulses which may be helpful here is the drowning swimmer's relation to the life-saver. The death-wish contradicts the life-wish in the drowning person. With his life-wish need he shouts for help. But with a death-wish, self-defeating, instinctive urge he reaches out and tries to grab the throat or head and shoulders of the saver-teacher who comes forward to him. If he succeeds, both the lifesaver and himself will come close to drowning, and may even drown.

The skilled life saver, of course, is trained to recognize this death-impulse and the grab-at-the-throat gesture, and dives under the floundering person to come up behind him. By momentarily surprising him in order to get him on his back, the hope is that the life-wish impulse will again assert itself and the drowning man will realize that this is his path to being saved. In a similar way the learner realizes that the path to learning is not argumentative resistance, but commitment to a trusting understanding of the creative teacher.

## ABANDONMENT OF THE SELF

Seen in this way, the path to learning is not aggressive resistance, but a kind of abandonment of oneself to the creative teacher (Stage I). Once this is done, the student, like the panic-stricken person, experiences security and confidence in the realization that the teacher does indeed know what he is doing, and that one can trust oneself to him. In this process then both the teacher and the learner are going safely into the threat of learning, as the person being pulled to the shore safely.

Thus genuine learning comes after a commitment to the learning experience in contrast to the death-instinct resistance which is self-defeating because one succeeds in impeding one's real impulses to learn. The person who resists is "peacefully" dead because he is the same as he was before: he has learned nothing. He has not changed. He has defeated learning because he submitted to the death-wish threat of change. In this sense he has negated Newman's expression that to grow is to change, and to grow really mature is to change often.

120

## MAN: A THEO-PSYCHOLOGICAL BEING

This leads to the conception that in order to justify the strength and power of the life instinct in man, we have to talk about the source of life-forces in psychological man. Psychological man, by definition, is oriented to death. In other words, one aspect of nature's wish for each man is that he be dead long before he is buried. This would be the best way to prepare him for what is his most evident end. In other words, those people might be thought to die best who have been dead a long time before the moment of physical death.

To justify the power of the life-instinct in man we have to consider nature as going beyond death in man. One way to define this is to say that man is a theo-psychological animal. By this we mean that man is not simply a being in the process of becoming: to say this is to say that what he is becoming is dead, and that his whole bent is towards death. That is the apparent goal of his natural becoming. But man is a being whose life-urge pushes him to a goal beyond death. It is this goal which explains his life-forces and validates the art and skill necessary in him and in others to bring these life-forces into fruition. By definition then we are talking about a beyond. And if we accept Eliade's definition that any going beyond the self is a kind of approach to God, then we are in a theo-psychological area. This would be our reason for calling this concept of the beyond in a man a theo-psychological definition of man.

Since nature leads man to death, there is a special effort required in man in his struggle to stay alive. It is not simply "natural" to him. We have here, in another form,

121

the profound decision of the Prodigal Son to turn and come back to his father. That is, a person does not have to respond to the life-impulse to return again to the source of life. He can defeat this, as the Prodigal Son could have defeated it. Or, using another biblical theme, in the horrible realism of the contrast between Peter and Judas, we see that Judas hanged himself, not because he was not sorry nor because he was not convinced of the meaning of Christ in his life, but because he could not stand the hatred that he had for himself in his own death-wish. The Gospel aptly describes this death-fulfillment in recording how Judas hanged himself. Peter's sorrow was not nearly as sharp nor as intense, but he had sufficient strength of life-impulse to turn and come back to face Christ. This is the difference between the two.

In summary, one aspect of satanism has been internalized in the death-wish. What spiritual writers have observed in man, psychologists have also observed and have given their own explanation. The death-instinct in a person would have him kill what is being created in another before it has the chance to emerge. He often does this by giving a destructive, negative response to the other, in place of genuinely understanding him. In each person there is some sort of balance between life and death, and if the person overcomes his own death-wish, he must still encounter the death-wish of the other, which in turn allies itself with his own and seeks to destroy life impulses. In destroying the other person, both are relieved of the threat of life. Death has a kind of "peace" as a cemetery surely is a "peaceful" place.

Thus anything which is alive in a person has two forces against it: his own and the other person's death-wish. But the very overcoming of one's own death-wish will threaten that of the other person, and his "peace" of death. He is therefore immediately threatened and impelled to some act to pervert and kill life. Nature, knowing that one's end is death, has prepared man to want death and to be comfortable and even at "peace" with it when he does not struggle for life.

## THE WILL-TO-POWER

Adler called this same thing the "will-to-power," and explained what happens when a person succeeds in communicating life. In his openness he seems to offer the other the power to destroy him. That is, once a person has opened himself to a life-urge expression, the other's will-to-power may not resist trying to crush him. Consequently the other will have to exercise a powerful control over his will-to-power to avoid acting out this destructive urge.

Other psychologists have used the term "self-defeating," and mean that the other, because of his will-to-power, or his death-wish, will seek to destroy any person who reveals himself, and he may well succeed. But in his very success he will himself suffer defeat because he thereby destroys himself. His own defeat is in death, since in death there is no self, and no extension beyond. There is nothing so alienating as death.

Thus the concepts of the will-to-power, the death-instinct, and self-defeat all describe the same solution that spiritual writers alluded to. There must come forward, on the part of the listener something which is not "natural" to him but something that, in a sense, is highly unnatural and something that all his inner forces are leagued against. By holding to life when he hears life, by holding to communion and community when he finds them, and by holding to his own self and embracing the self of the other, he is doing something in a way unnatural because it is beyond himself.

## CONCLUSION

It is here that we see the meaning in the concept of the art and skill of listening, the art and skill of the listening heart. This is not something that is natural, as we proposed, but something against which all of one's natural forces are leagued. Unless the person has some reassurance that the listener has some skill to make a warm, understanding, affective, cognitive, incarnate, creative, redemptive relationship possible, he is a fool to take the risk of being open. He is a fool to risk his openness to the chance tenacious death-wishes of the other. For the listener to give the other such reassurance demands the highest art of communication of his open, warm, receptive self to him. At the same time it demands skill in both affectively understanding the person when he makes the communication and also a profound cognitive skill which enables the person, by adequate linguistic symbols and cognition, to abstract and reflect on the "why" of his feelings. So, little by little, he arrives at an increasing grasp, not only of a security feeling with himself, but also a genuine knowledge of himself or "gnosis."

Through the incarnately redemptive, cognitive symbolizations by the listener of the affective world of the speaker, a person is able to arrive at the "why" of his affects and the subtle implicit and explicit self-investments and personal value systems that they contain.

# VI. The Dynamics of Prayer

CONSIDERING how man relates to others, and in a special religious sense how he relates to God, reveals a great similarity between those two relationships. Directly related to God—defined as a total Other and as a complete mystery beyond man—there can be no human or anthropological model or comparison. But given a commitment to God and the assurance of divine love and redemption, a comparison is possible. The conditions that a man faces in himself as he proposes to himself a commitment to God are not dissimilar to those conditions when he thinks of committing himself, in faith, trust, hope, and love, to another person.

## THE LEAP OF FAITH

The most basic aspect of a man's faith in God is the belief that God really cares about him; that he has worth and value in God's eyes. This belief must be communicated to man by some kind of divine promise, relayed either, as in the Christian tradition, by God having become incarnate, or, in other traditions, by some prophet who speaks God's word. There is no intrinsic reason why man necessarily should believe that God cares about him. The Greek notion of Fates and of a Force behind the universe indifferent to man, or at least completely removed from human concern, conceived of a Deity without such personal human concern.

Consequently, the first act of faith that anyone makes is not simply that God exists as a Force behind the universe, or even as some kind of ultimate goal for himself. The first belief and commitment that one must make as he thinks of his relationship with God, is to accept with conviction the fact that God genuinely cares about him. This must be accompanied by a belief that his unique individual self has a special value and significance in God's eyes. He must be willing to accept and give an affirmative answer to St. Paul's question, "Know you not that you were bought by a great price?", that we have repeatedly referred to.

The way a man relates to God will ultimately depend on how he relates to others. Yet this is not to be confused with an anthropomorphic conception of God. Before one can make the "leap" to God, he has to somehow know that God cares about him and loves him. There is nothing within him which says this has to be so. Not even the logic of the cosmos can give the reassurance that God cares. Rather, it requires another person's love in a human relationship. Only this can communicate to man the possibility that God loves him. And only this will enable him to make the "leap."

## CARE FOR THE PERSON IN HIMSELF

The same conditions are necessary for one person to believe in another. The barriers to belief in another are encountered most openly in counseling and psychotherapeutic relationships. But this is often evident in family life, for example between parents and children, or husband and wife. The main barrier is the unwillingness to trust others. It constitutes one of the most characteristic elements in a person's alienation, loneliness and withdrawal and is most commonly behind a need for counseling therapy. Because of experiences in earlier life, particularly with parents and those close to him as a child, such a person has never been sure that anyone really cared about him. The resulting insecurity can exist even in the face of extrinsic protestations of love and concern from parents and friends, particularly in the form of expenditures of gifts and material symbols. Yet this can fail to convey to the person that he is honestly of worth and has real meaning. Frequently, as a result of such an attempt to show concern and love, one will feel himself manipulated and maneuvered for the other person's purpose, and of no real value or significance in himself.

With this kind of background then, the person understandably comes to counseling-therapy with suspicion and insecurity. It is difficult for him to believe that even the counselor-therapist might care for him and genuinely be concerned for him. Such a person is so deeply convinced that others find him of meaning only when they can use and manipulate him for their own purposes that it is quite difficult for him to accept anything that might make him openly trust or bind himself to them.

In such a condition, then, his first and most basic "leap" is out of himself, out of his suspicion of others, out of the anxiety that he will only be manipulated, and out of his feeling of self-worthlessness and his urge to escape. To do this he must first be convinced that at least one person—in this case, the counselor-therapist—could genuinely care for him for himself.

Sometimes one's initial commitment and its significance is shown in quite touching ways. We can give two illustrations of this. In her book *Play Therapy,** Virginia Axline

*Virginia Axline, *Play Therapy*, New York, 1969.

127

discusses a child who came to her after school because he was in difficulty and conflict with a number of his teachers. Somewhere in the middle of the sessions, when he felt himself becoming engaged and committed to the counselor, he suddenly stopped, turned abruptly to her, and said in great concern and confusion, "I don't get it—I don't get it. I don't get into your hair. I don't cause you any trouble. I'm not . . . I'm not any kind of a pain in the neck to you. What are you spending this time with me for? What are you getting out of it? Well, what are you doing this for?"

Here we see the strange, almost mysterious, sense of a child's insecurity that someone would honestly care for him, rather than be concerned only to correct him and to make him behave better so that he would not be a nuisance to them in a class. We see the mystery of the child's amazement that someone could genuinely care for him in himself and not simply because he is a "behavior problem" and needs "taking care of."

To give another example, a man, after a period of counseling therapy, was discussing with the counselor his surprising experience in going to church the previous Sunday and hearing a sermon about the love of God. Up to this point he had not been a religious man, but he sometimes accompanied his family simply for propriety's sake. His background was that of a stern, rigid, father and a passive mother from neither of whom he had ever felt any kind of genuine love. He knew only fear towards his father and a confused distance and alienation from his mother, as well as a certain resentment that she simply submitted to the father and never saw his side. In view of this, as he described it, the love of God had never previously had any meaning for him. Insofar as he could

128

think of God at all, he had to conceive of Him only in the stern, rigid terms of his experience with his father. His amazement, expressed to the counselor, hinged around the fact that, while the sermon on the love of God had been a routine and not particularly distinguished one, he found himself understanding for the first time and feeling in a conscious and genuine way that it might be truly possible for him to believe that God could love him. For the first time he could think of himself as actually possessing and committing himself to a religious belief in a God that cared for him.

In discussing this with the counselor, he slowly came to the awareness that the only possible experience that could account for this change in his attitude towards a loving God was the one he was then having with the counselor. As he put it, "You know me better than any other person has ever known me. You know me with all my weaknesses and inadequacies and all the things that I would be ashamed to have most people know about me. I have told this to you and yet I have come away time after time with the conviction that none of this in any way vitiates your deep positive regard for me, your respect for me as a person, and your reflecting my sense of special unique worth for you. I believe more than anything else that it is this experience with you which, if I may, I will call love, that allows me now for the first time in my life to begin to feel that I could genuinely trust in and possibly commit myself to a belief in a God who could love me."

In these two illustrations we see that trusting the unconditional positive regard of the counselor is similar to, if not identical with, the first religious faith commitment. For here one has to make a commitment in a God who is not a blind force, or simply Fate, indifferent to

129

man's destiny. It is a "leap" towards a God who personally cares for each person in all the unique aspects of his own personal identity and need.

Just as there is no absolutely compelling reason, then, to believe that God cares about oneself, there is also no such reason to believe that other people care either. This is often seen in the relationship of parents to children where parents do not communicate love to the child simply by giving him many external things. In fact, this may convey to the child that he was simply manipulated or used for the other person's sake. As we have seen, there is a sense of wonderment when a child realizes that somebody really cares about him for himself. Likewise there is the amazement of a man, realizing that somebody knows all about him and still has not rejected him.

It is this leap of trust in the other then that makes it possible for a person to place some kind of trust in a loving God. Prior to trusting another person the notion of a loving God is quite difficult. It is therefore through belief in another person that one is able to make the "leap" towards God or even to propose to oneself the possibility of that "leap."

## THE POSSIBILITY OF TOTAL COMMITMENT

Once this possibility is advanced then, as in a human relationship, the measure of trust in God, and in God's promised love and care, is determined by the person himself. He may invest only to a limited degree, as he might in a person whom he begins to trust such as a counselor towards whom he is still insecure; or he may make a far more complete commitment of himself. In the same way, a man determines the amount, the intensity and the degree of commitment and abandonment that he will make to a God whom he accepts as a Person who loves

130

him and sees his unique personal worth. The quality and extent of redemption is, in this sense, an operant of faith. One gets out of a faith experience just what he puts into it. This is true of relationships with other people—marriage, for example. It is true of counseling therapy and it seems therefore also true of one's relationship with God. The intensity and profundity of one's commitment and the concomitant results are in the hands of the person himself, if one assumes a belief in the promises and assurances of a divine Being who has loved first, in the statement of St. John's Gospel.

It is the person himself who determines to what degree he will commit himself and the extent of his commitment. He also, therefore, determines the extent of his redemption. The unconditional and total commitment to God would also seem to imply total redemption. One may commit himself in degrees to others, and to the ultimate Other, but then the extent to which he is redeemed is also limited. And if one never makes any commitment, then he remains in isolation.

Following upon this would be the actual faith commitment to God. Interwoven with such a faith commitment is both trust and hope. The Greeks, in their concept of order in the cosmos, and in their notion of an intelligent Force behind the universe, still saw only a faint relationship between God and man. In this context, they understandably saw hope, not only as unwise and foolish, but even as dangerous and vicious for man. For if the Fates had predetermined, in an indifferent and perhaps frivolous way, an individual's goal and purpose, then his wise decision is simply to abandon himself to what the events of life seem to indicate is going to happen to him. Greek drama is filled with this kind of passive submission, almost like the passive submission of Michelangelo's statue called

131

"Captive," where the figure lets itself be lulled and controlled by the bands which tie it. In such a view, there is no conscious aggressive free struggle of self-assertion and self-affirmation in the face of the universe. There is simply an abandonment to a final meaninglessness for which hope would be vicious and even sinful. Hope would be sinful and vicious because it would be tragically misleading and disillusioning. Things are the way they are with no possibility of man overcoming them.

## MUTUAL COMMITMENT IN THE RELATIONSHIP

In a world of Fates, a hopeful song or rallying-cry, such as "We Shall Overcome," would be inconceivable. Trust and hope are only possible in a context of belief in a God who cares personally about one in his unique and individual existence. Trust and hope are only possible if, in some mysterious way, one's response to the caring of another and his investment in it would affect one's own condition. Unless one sees that the measure of investment of himself in a relationship, whether it be therapy or marriage or a genuine friendship, has consequences of significance to the outcome of that relationship, then trust and hope are meaningless. If the relationship is pre-determined, then, at best, it is the action of puppets or actors acting out a pre-determined scenario. It is not any kind of creative self-affirmation.

What counseling, marriage, or friendship at their best imply is that much depends finally on what both people commit to the relationship. On the basis that one of them, as in the case of the therapist, has made a genuine commitment that can be believed in and trusted, then the measure of what will be achieved from the relationship is determined by the intensity and extension of the return

132

commitment and gift of self on the part of the other person.

One's commitment to God parallels this, given a belief in and an acceptance of a loving God who is genuinely concerned for each one of us personally. What finally determines the end effect of of the commitment would be the intensity with which one trusts and hopes in the outcome of the relationship as truly fulfilling the promises and the significance that the Divine communication has set forth. One must believe in such a way that trust and hope follow; this is what will make possible any final and adequate fruition in the relationship.

Basic to any commitment then, is trust and hope. While the Greeks had the notion of abandonment, it was an abandonment without hope and without trust, since one cannot have trust and hope in an uncaring Fate. Hope and trust are made possible by a belief in a loving God. This is similar to any friendship between two people. The relationship will be determined by their willingness to trust and hope in it, rather than seeing it as some pre-determined situation over which they have no control. The trust and hope then that they put into the relationship will determine its creativity.

## THE PLACE OF LOVE

Love is in the bond, or the deep channel of intense communion which follows from this kind of trusting and hoping. It follows from a belief in the promises and assurances of another that one is genuinely loved for one's self. Only with that secure assurance can one give himself in peace. Peace then is not only the tranquility of order, as Augustine made famous, but it is at the same time a surcease of restlessness, insecurity and questioning. It is a coming-to-rest in, through, and with the open acceptance and understanding of the other person. Stated in the analogy of the trapeze act, it is that moment when, having made the leap off the secure swing, one is going through the air and hands touch other hands and are firmly grasped so that one feels one's self securely held and sustained by the firm grip of a friend. Whether this happens in counseling therapy, in marriage, or in any other type of deep friendship, it is such moments that we would describe as the zenith-moments of both loving and being loved.

Related to God, the moment when Love occurs between God and man is that moment when a man, in belief and trust and hope, makes a final gift of himself, a final "leap" out of himself, a final letting-go of all those self-protective and self-encapsulating urges that keep him bound. He trusts totally and completely in the assurances of a Divine Being that he is genuinely loved. Like the birds of the air or the flowers in the field he is truly the object of Divine care and concern. This is the love-gift that sets up the state of communion and community between God and man. Hope and trust, then, are concomitant with love.

## DYNAMISM WITHIN THE RELATIONSHIP

The occurrence of love in commitment might seem to be the final assurance that nothing else need matter. From a static or purely abstractive point of view this might, in fact, appear to be so. In reality, however, if one considers the nature of man and the transient condition of his impulses, then such a static attitude rather tends towards death than towards life. One sees this in human relations. At the very moment when people begin to take one another for granted, whether in marriage or in friendship, or in any other genuine relationship, there emerges a kind of chilled

134

air that is like the death-air of sepulchres. For, to take love for granted and to assume that what has been established must of necessity remain like a kind of concretized, materialized structure, as one might think of a large building once it has been built, is to miss the living, moving and constant going-out quality that is necessary to fulfillment in the human condition.

One might, for example, conceive of community as an orderly, planned and rigidly designed city. But then there would be something that, in its very fixity and determination, is itself inhuman and not alive. The living human condition is constantly moving and, therefore, constantly needs to be re-defined and re-asserted. It needs to be constantly renewed or it dies. Life is not like a static structure that stands some place and stays there. Life is constantly developing its resources, like the tree receiving nourishment from the earth and spreading out into the atmosphere around it. The human relationship that centers on a static definition of love has already, by that definition, contradicted love and given clues that love is diminishing or has even disappeared. The façade of love may still be there but in fact it may be a dead, rather than a living, relationship.

Consequently, the words "communion" and "communication" are basic to a genuine living sense of community between persons. Without continued struggle to communicate one to the other, to understand, to share, to strive to get to know one another better, to try to penetrate the mystery of the other, without constant experience of hope and trust in the other, and continual communication around such experience, without consistant renewal of hope and trust, love itself is in danger of losing its strength and of ultimately dying.

## THE NECESSITY OF PRAYER

Essential to the continued relationship of love between man and God is prayer. For as communication, seen as understanding, sharing, trusting, participating, and seeking to penetrate mystery, is fundamental to human relationships and to a deepening of human belonging, so prayer, as a communication of man to God, must necessarily be continually renewed and deepened. In the search and struggle to share more and so to participate more in the friendship of God, and in the increasingly greater trust and abandonment to God, comes an even deeper sense of the validity of faith, hope, and love in God. This represents the traditional notion of "believing that one may understand" and the elements by which such understanding proceeds from belief and through prayer. A person trusts all the unique aspects of himself to God. He trusts, hopes in, and abandons himself to God's listening ear and profoundly personal caring response.

We see here a similarity to the trust in the listening ear that the client must make to the counselor-therapist. The client speaks of himself. His basic security and openness depends on the degree to which he trusts the deep understanding concern of the counselor. Out of confidence in this concern and his own struggle to communicate, he gains in his understanding of himself. This then enlargens his relationship with others and his trust, hope and capacity to give himself in love.

## THE NATURE OF PRAYER

Prayer is then the continual communication of the self in all the subtleties of one's uniqueness, depth, and mystery, much as one would communicate one's self to an intensely

136

sensitive counselor or, even more commonly, to a genuinely understanding and trustworthy friend. There is no limit to the degree to which the person in prayer opens himself up and unfolds himself and so communes with God. This kind of total communion and unrestricted trust of the self in communication with God constitute the essential aspects of prayer. Therefore, to arrive at a state of love with God is not enough. It must be continually verified by prayer. A static condition is a contradiction to life itself since life is continually moving onward, is dynamic. Similar to the relationship with God without prayer, as soon as two people take one another for granted, love dies. They must continually struggle in communication to penetrate the mystery of the other.

Just as the counselor gives the client his ear and the client is trusting the counselor to understand him, so man can be seen as the "client" and God as the "counselor." In this way man is struggling to communicate with God in prayer in order to be understood. It is as he gains a profound sense of being understood that he is in communion with and one with God.

## PRAYER AS THERAPY

One might go a step further and talk about a therapeutic of prayer. Communication with the other, and all the conditions of faith, confidence, hope, and love that we have described have, in counseling and psychotherapeutic experience, increasingly proved helpful. The same consequences might be proposed with even greater and more extensive results in man's communion and communication with God. This seems to be an ancient idea which in some measure has been lost. Augustine, we said, used the Greek word "*therapeia*" for his concept of grace. That is, he conceived of the relationship between God and man

137

not simply as a gift from God to man, as the Latin word "*gratia*" would imply, but also as a cure, as a healing of man. In God was the final solace for man's restlessness, incompleteness, and inadequacy, and for the primitive condition of anxiety that seems to be intrinsic to humanity itself. In this context, the familiar phrase "care of souls," which in Latin would be "*cura animarum*," is rightly identified with the work of religion and of religious ministration as a "cure." The Greek derivative of this would be "psycho-therapy."

If we parallel man's communion with God to the client's communion with the counselor, or the patient's communion with the therapist, and if we consider the healing, wholesome salvation implied in this communication, then prayer has even greater significance for man. In the "angst" of the human condition, in the constant turmoil of movement and transition and change, in the constant loss as well as gain of those things on which man immediately and in time sets his heart, there are, at every moment in human experience, stages of disillusionment, discouragement, loss of confidence, threat, fear of failure, cowardice, and withdrawal. Augustine saw this as the human condition. He saw it first of all, and perhaps most profoundly, in himself. He threw himself on God and out of this sense of commitment and confidence and assurance, he drew not only communion and communication but, in a very literal sense, therapy.

This notion is contained in the word "salvation" and, as well, in the word "holy" which is, at the same time, the Saxon word, "wholeness." We have lost the therapeutic element in man's relationship with God by being focused primarily on creedal commitments and on the quality of removal that terms like "supernatural" suggest in their

138

THE DYNAMICS OF PRAYER

effort to describe God's uniqueness and complete difference from man. In fact, however, if we accept, as the
religious man must, a divine promise of caring and commitment similar to, but immeasurably greater than, the
commitment of the counselor or therapist to a person,
then within the trust and belief in one's genuine capacity
to commune with God according to the human manner
that one would communicate with friends, one has in the
Divine relationship of prayer, the most profound kind of
human therapy.

The richness of counseling and psychotherapy in unfolding for us the benefits that emerge when one person
trusts and unreservedly communicates in and through
another, can also reveal in a fresh way something of what is
meant by the assurance, "Ask and you shall receive, seek
and you shall find." The same assurance is found in the
simple but profound communication from God to man
that "because she has loved much, much is forgiven her";
or, in another context, "thy faith hath made thee whole."
These are statements not only of communion and of
response from God back to man as a result of man's
deeply trusting and loving commitment and communication; they are also statements of therapy, of cure, of
becoming whole again, addressed to man's "angst" and to
his segmented and disintegrated state.

Prayer has profound significance in the dynamic of
man's state of "angst," of his state of restlessness, of his
complete inability to save himself finally and his need not
only of others in the deepest friendship or in the therapeutic relationship, but even more ultimately, of his basic
need of God. Prayer then would be a confident believing,
hoping, trusting, and loving communication between God
and man. The basis of speaking of a therapeutic of prayer

139

is Augustine's identity of grace with therapy. If a human relationship of therapy between client and counselor has such value, how much more so would be such a relationship, if it were established, between man and God? This would be the ultimate significance of a therapy of prayer.

## BEYOND DEATH

We therefore must think of the death-wish as tending to keep man encapsulated in his own ego. He is reluctant to trust his own self, and, even more, to trust others. By vaulting out of such restrictions, the ego moves towards trusting its whole self. The different somatic, instinctive, emotional functions of the organism can then be integrated with a broader, higher self-wisdom. This is a greater movement towards life and life's meaning. It can lead to commitment to others and finally to the Total Other. If death is the immediate goal of man, then there is nothing in one's commitment to any other except the Total Other—God—that can lead one beyond the portal of death. Consequently, even human communication, redemptive and life-giving as it is, in friendship, in marriage, in family life, and when necessary, in counseling therapy, faces a final frustration and incapacity for which the death-instinct aptly prepares it. For even human friendship at its most intense, and at its fullest life component, faces inevitable death.

For man to be truly and genuinely alive and not caught up in self-deception, it is not enough that he trust himself and others. To believe in, have hope in, and love himself and others—these are simply preludes and prologues. These, of themselves, still end in death and the touch of death is on them. To make the life impulses have significance beyond himself, others and death, man must engage

140

himself in dialogue, commitment, and abandonment to the Total Other. This is the only door that opens beyond death. All others are locked to man and make him finally captive in a "no-exit" world. It is faith, hope, and love of God, in a continuing communion and dialogue, that is both life-giving and therapeutic. This is the dialogue that we call prayer.

Such a commitment to God, therefore, is most consistent with a man's struggle to believe in, hope, and love himself as a whole person and to love others. Faith, hope, and love of God are a fitting culmination of a life that believes in and trusts itself and others, and so emerges out to hope and love in an unfolding which goes beyond death. This is the final therapy of prayer which no human therapy can achieve.

Consequently, the using of one's life-forces to go out of one's self towards others is limited because in doing so one still does not get beyond death. But to engage one's own life-forces with one's self and others, in addition to its rich immediate meaning, can be a stepping stone towards engaging one's life forces with God. This requires acts of faith, hope, and love beyond man. It involves living in communion, communication, and community with God. This is man's sustaining strength and the ultimate therapeutic for the "angst" of the human condition.

## PRAYER OF PETITION

Once the religious bind with God has been accepted, one of the things that follows is the nature of the communication itself with God. Such communication we generally call prayer, at least one form of it. A consideration of God and the nature of God, however, reveals that prayer is both an approach to God and a means of honoring and giving to Him the true recognition of His being. One would give such recognition to any genuine friend who deserves honor and respect.

God, however, does not need our prayers. But the reverse is most fundamental. Man faced with the unknown and the unanswerable, with confusions and conflicts, needs prayer. He has need of this very special relationship in order to communicate his difficulties in the assurance that he will be understood. He does this in the way that a friend can communicate with the realization and faith-conviction that God can be truly helpful and so his prayer will bring aid and comfort. Consequently, prayer of petition takes the form of asking God for help in a time of need and personal concern. This implies a *personal* relationship. All religions emphasize this but particularly the Judaeo-Christian religions. One sees this clearly in the highly personal relationship between God and man that is expressed in the Psalms. One sees it also in the repeated emphasis of such statements as "Ask and ye shall receive, seek and ye shall find, knock and it shall be opened unto you." One feels the great peace and reassurance in Christ's comparison of our lives in the hand of God as being like "the birds of the air and the lilies of the field." This leads to a state of security through prayer and the right of man in need to seek God's help.

It also faces a fundamental existential condition of man, a fundamental reality, namely, that often there is no answer to the conflict and confusion of his life except in prayer. In Lincoln's words, "One often goes down on one's knees because there is nowhere else to go."

The relationship to God in prayer, then, is one in which the person himself genuinely needs God as he needs friends. The nature of the petition to God would have all the elements and meaning of that between friends, and

142

much more besides. Yet this petitioning does not imply any precise solving or clear cut answers to problems or to conflicts. It is more that it is a genuine need and if one believes and so accepts and lives a religious commitment, one turns to God. This does not mean giving up. Rather, in Augustine's terms, one acts as if everything depended on oneself but one prays because one believes everything finally depends on God.

It is in the nature of friendship that a friend is not only one who understands but is also available with personal help in time of need. Consequently, in our binding relationship with God, trust also includes the capacity and willingness of God to aid us in the time of need and so to offer special and particular help in answer to our petition. It is in this sense that one prays not only to give honor and respect due the unique and special friendship between man and God, but also to seek God's help as well.

## PRAYER: A MODEL OF FRIENDSHIP

The Lord's Prayer, as a model of all prayer, catches this well. It begins with the respectful regard of God as a source of man's being and it ends as any friendship-communication in a time of need would end. There is a petition for help and the reassurance that, as a true and genuine friend, one can expect God's understanding ear and helping hand. One goes to a friend with the reassurance and peace of knowing that he will get some kind of help, that there will be aid and even resolution of conflict if he can genuinely trust in that relationship. So it would be in petition to God. It is possible there too that if we believe, we could rely on finding solace and healing. Such a friendship relies on seeking God out in our needs.

It would be a poor friend indeed, who, having the capacity to help and having at hand the remedies, would

143

not offer them to his friend. Consequently, since our belief and trust in God imitates the form of human friendship, then we can include in it the same kind of confident and open seeking of help from God that we would normally include in any genuine friendship. To whom can one turn if not to friends? If our bind and bond with God is a belief in a genuine friendship, then these same things, in greater extent and purpose, obviously are included in the belief in and trust in man's divine friendship.

## MEDITATION: SEEKING TO UNDERSTAND

Following from this is the process by which one thinks about, and relates to a friend. One would follow the same process with God. This is generally called religious meditation. By meditation is meant the seeking to understand the actions of God, and man's cooperation. This is particularly applicable to the Christian religion in its focus on the life of Christ and the personages surrounding Christ. Meditation, in this sense, consists in trying to penetrate the meaning and significance of these actions with the intent of applying them to one's self. This implies that the actions of God in relationship to man, like the actions of a friend to a friend, have deep and lasting significance.

Thought and study are necessary before the complicated meanings of a friend's actions can be thoroughly understood. In much the same manner, one thinks about, studies out, and seeks an ever deeper understanding of the meaning of God's actions with regard to man. In a special way meditation focuses on their significance for the person himself. These actions of God have special personal application.

Meditation, then, might be seen as the attempt of one

friend to understand the significance of the actions of another. The significance may not be clear at the time, but an important element in the relationship is a trust that the significance will be more evident in the subsequent thinking through the action and so revealing the message it carries. This would be a mediative process.

## CONTEMPLATION

There is however one further and final relationship with God which, when achieved, is the most profound of all. Using a human model to catch the intensity of this we must go to the relationship of lovers. It is quite evident to anyone in love, or to people who are used to one another over years of love, that a sense of presence is perhaps the most significant thing about their relationship. It is neither talking to one another, nor even helping one another nor, finally, even studying the significance of one another's actions or communications that is the richest and deepest awareness that they have together. It is rather the many hours they can spend in silent awareness of one another's presence and in the security and meaning of that presence and the strength and solace that it gives.

Parents are aware of this with the sense of the presence of the children in the home. Husband and wife are aware of it in their sense of one another's presence or absence. Young lovers find their deepest communication not in talking but in holding hands and feeling the fresh and exciting reassurance of the presence of the other caring person. Something of these human experiences lead the way for the same kind of belief and trust in the sense of God's presence in a person's life.

The experience of divine contemplation would be captured in those human experiences of the quiet reassurance of one another and the silent remembrance of past inti-

145

mate experiences together, of deep sharing and deep commitments. What this amounts to is a kind of filtering down to the essence of all the other communications and qualities in a relationship. It is that final element of complete reassurance. This involves not only the security of the presence of that person, but the total openness of the person to the deepest understanding and acceptance of the other at every level of his being. This reflects his worth and meaning and so is redemptive of him.

In relationship to God this demands a kind of silent time between man and God. It is a period of final letting go on man's part and complete abandonment of himself to God. This is the moment—sometimes a very long moment—of contemplation.

## THE ULTIMATE LEAP

We have seen that in the relationship of the ego to the self there has to be a kind of trust which involves a letting go and commitment to other parts of the self in order to enable the ego to relate to them in a more integrated way. Before such integration can occur, the ego must trust the whole self so as to be freed from anxiously narrowed defenses and threat reactions. Such open trusting commitment allows the ego to fuse into and to incorporate the whole person.

We saw too that this is equally true in friendship with another person. In the manner of the trapeze act, one must take the jump, being assured that hands will be extended out to save him from a fall. This kind of Kierkegaardian leap and letting go is also necessary to divine contemplation. The person's faith in his life allows him to let himself go into God. He can leap out of the constricted limits of his narrowed anxious self and abandon himself in the total security that the reaching hands of God will always catch him and sustain him.

Perhaps no expression defines more profoundly this process than that of, "He that shall lose his life shall save it." At the height of contemplation one loses his life in giving himself up in the meaning of God in his life. But he comes back redeemed and fulfilled at a level not possible through his own human activity. The same freeing one's self, and the self to others, is magnified here. From the total giving-up of the self to God could come a kind of secure trust in and integration of the self not humanly possible otherwise.

## AWARENESS OF LIMITS

David Bakan has spoken of the agentic and nonagentic forces in man. Using these terms, contemplation would be the maximizing of nonagentic forces. It would be the giving over of one's self to an intelligent force and loving person in whom all things find their fulfillment and meaning. The experience of a small child's hand trustingly resting in that of an adult as they walk across the street, or the peaceful security of the blind person in one who sees, would suggest this total, peaceful security at its most profound level between friend and divine friend.

Cardinal Newman saw something of this kind of contemplative trust in his "Lead Kindly Light" amid the encircling gloom. It is a sense of never being without final meaning and significance in the universe because of one's nonagentic resting in the hands of God. It is the way the trapeze artist rests in the hands of the one who catches him, or the child securely rests in the arms of the parent, or the blind person securely rests in being led by the one who sees, extended through time to eternity. Darkness and incapacity are not threatening to these persons. They have made a total commitment in trust to another and therefore they are assured of strength and support.

Man must be non-agentic in those things beyond the limits of himself because he cannot control them. Finally only God's sustaining strength can support him. But in those things where he has the power to assert himself and determine action, the supportive strength of God heightens and encourages him to commit himself to such actions. In the anxiety, narrowness and insecurity that are evident even in those things where a man has determination, he can tend to fear to take the risk of plunging outward. Even there he must often have a special courage to open himself up to realize the fulfillment of his own capacity to self-determination and self-affirmation. This commitment of himself to God allows man securely to experience his own limits. In knowing his own limits, he can know where to place his trust and his faith. From this comes the courage increasingly to be able to go into action towards all goals within his own power. He is encouraged to fulfill himself to his limits because of the sustaining power that the relationship of God gives him.

## APPROACHES TO CONTEMPLATION

Through the ages various methods or approaches to contemplation have been devised. They all have as their intent the placing of the self in the presence of God, as one would trustfully feel the presence of a friend. They also demand the letting go of one's self, like the trapeze act, into God's hands and feeling the security of the abiding presence and supporting strength of God.

One of the most familiar approaches to contemplation takes the form of invoking the presence of God in the Latin word *"video."* "I see" strongly affirms to one's self

148

the presence of God's friendship, warmth and understanding, much as a blind person might affirm "seeing"
the presence he senses. The "*video*" suggests the idea of a
faith commitment cutting through one's blindness and
recognizing God's presence even if one does not physically see him. Held for some time, this "seeing" reinforces
and relaxes the person. He is with a friend and they are in
silent communion with one another. One is blind. He
senses the friend's presence not by any speech, touch or
action, but simply by the faith-awareness that his friend is
there. This kind of intense sense of the presence of God
the Latin word "video" is intended to invoke.

The second process is a personalization of the awareness
of Divine presence in the person's own needs. The Latin
word "*sitio*" embodies this. It is intended to denote the
thirsting appetite for God, much as the line in the Psalms,
"as the heart panteth after the fountains of living waters."
In this way the person thirsts after God's purposive
fulfillment of himself. Consequently, in the deep and
profound awareness of God's presence there is at the same
time a second phase. This is the need, like the thirsting
man approaching the oasis, that the person in the human
condition feels once he is caught up in the intensity of
God's presence.

The parallel here is to the physical thirst for water. But
it could also be carried over to the Augustinian restlessness and the goal-less feeling that no particular aim or
purpose in life can totally satisfy or fulfill the yearnings
that man has. The time spent in the thirst for God and
recognizing that one has arrived at the oasis and is in the
presence of the fountain of living waters—this is the intent
of the contemplative awareness of "*sitio*" or thirst. It is
the slaking of one's thirsting needs at the Divine fountain.

The first approach to contemplation would be as a blind

149

man who senses the presence of a friend; in the second a person is aware of his basic personal needs and knows that he is at the only place where he can have those needs fulfilled.

## NEED OF SELF-FULFILLMENT

At no time is the nonagentic commitment to God so total that one is not also involved in one's own agentic responsibility and determination to the maximum of his capacity. This notion is contained in the term *"volo"*—"I will" or "I wish."

The importance of man's will in his own commitment to himself and in his respect and regard for all the positive potential that he is capable of, is here strongly emphasized. One's agentic forces come forward even as one's self in the secure hands of divine friendship. But this does not relieve man of the necessity of maximizing his own best fulfillment of himself in and through God.

Hence, rather than contemplation and the resultant security in God's Divine support and strength leading man away from self-affirmation, it rather could be said to lead him to it. It is the anxious, fearful man, confused and unable to free himself of the sense of surrounding threat, who is apt to remove himself most from others. It is he who, in his isolated desperation, is afraid of letting himself go and committing himself to his total integrated self, to others and to God.

The more secure one is in the Divine presence, strength and support, the freer he is to maximize his own total potential of self-affirmation and fulfillment. It is this very special, self-determining capacity, even in the contemplative abandonment to God, that the theme *"volo"* highlights and defines.

In such total abandonment, instead of being relieved

150

from his responsibilities, man is genuinely freed to determine what he can do. This works positively to move him forward. In no sense does it take away from him the determination of how he is going to move. But with such security behind him, he can do whatever he must to fulfill his own being. He is not the stagnated victim of narrow, alienated anxiety.

## THE STRENGTHENING OF SELF-AFFIRMATION

Counseling and psycho-therapy have revealed that as one grows to understand the process of maturing and developing more fully his own capacities, he recognizes a need for both the secure support of another and the freedom for self-affirmation and determination. To take the person over, direct his life, control him and determine for him the ends and purposes of his immediate actions and more ultimate goals, is to rob him of a growth force and strength that he needs for his own maturity and adult identity. Consequently, terms like "non-directive" and "client-centered" emerged to highlight the element of an understanding relationship that was supportive and deeply helpful to the person but still let him free. In this understanding, strengthening relationship every effort was made to allow for the person's own affirmation of himself and his own direction towards the goals and purposes that he himself saw emerging out of his deeper trust in and understanding of himself.

In an even greater way then, contemplation and the sense of God's presence still leaves a man free. Supported as he feels by the Divine Counselor, he can face the unknown, indeterminate elements, and the mystery of his life. But the assurance of God's presence heightens, as in the human counseling relationship, the freedom of self-affirmation and personal identity of the person.

151

Like any friendship, then, personal relationship to God does not rob the person of his identity and self-determination but rather heightens and furthers them. The presence of God behind such self-meaning, emphasized in the thematic focus of *"volo,"* is a heightening and strengthening force that makes even more evident the unique identity of the person and his capacity to will his best fulfillment of himself. In counseling and psychotherapy the emphasis was to maintain the integrity of the person and his gradual growth in the responsible taking-over of his own life. By parallel, the secure relationship with God does not impinge on a person's unique meaning and identity. On the contrary, it is this that permits him to have integrity and so aim at more complete human fulfillment of all he is and can be.

## THE LIMITS OF MAN

Much as friendship with another predetermines the limits of the self by invoking the limits of the other, so the contemplative sense of the presence of God invokes an awareness of each man's own limits. This is symbolized in the words *"volo tecum"*—"I will," or "wish with you."

Such Divine awareness reveals the limitations and inadequacies of even the clearest of human visions and intentions. The human will is therefore best affirmed through trust and security in broader and far more extensive desire of self-fulfillment in and through God. A man can trust that a wise, understanding and concerned friend wishes to act only in and through his own best self-determination. His wisdom, however, is verified not by contradicting another but by seeing farther and wider where his friend's real goal leads him. So one wishes one's best self-fulfillment through relying on the greater per-

152

sonal meaning and purpose that the Divine relationship will eventually unfold.

A person in contemplation always wishes as much as he can his own most complete fulfillment. But he wishes it with a deep realization of the limitations of his own awareness and of his capacity to wish well and adequately for himself. Trusting to the secure presence and concern of God, the person invokes this wish in and through a more extensive and more ultimately effective wish for him of the Divine Other. While man wills to fulfill himself, he does so in and through God. He believes, and contemplation strengthens his belief that in and through abandoning himself to God in a clear recognition of his own limits he will be most adequately fulfilled as a person.

## COMMUNICATION IN MYSTERY

The four themes, *"video," "sitio," "volo"* and *"volo tecum"* are means of affirming and experiencing the presence of God as one might experience a friend. But this is done through faith affirmation in "darkness." One has to commit one's self to the realization of this presence when there are no sense clues of such a presence. The most important aspect of contemplation is the necessity of abandonment, trust, and total commitment which leads to a kind of knowing or experiencing in darkness. To prepare for this commitment often requires deep self-purification. This has been made famous particularly by St. John of the Cross in his expression "the dark night of the soul." He reasoned that, faced with the actual presence of God, man's understanding is blinded and paralyzed, much as one's eyes could be blinded by too close a look at an extremely bright light or at the sun. So, experiencing God comes in such a "darkness" of understanding.

The very intensity of divine illumination can overwhelm human understanding as light can overwhelm the eyes. The direct communion between man and God could occur in the mystery and in the darkness of the unknown. This would be very different from conscious communicative language, such as that expressed by the prophets or Christ, adjusted as this was to a human mode of communication and understanding.

As the mystics emphasize, within the darkness there is a kind of luminosity and understanding which surpasses all understanding. This sense of all things finding their ultimate meaning and fulfillment in and through God is intangible and not definable in human terms. It is a mystery therefore not communicable in a limited degree in the language of poetry and extended analogy. If we believe in the writings of mystics, we believe they are witnesses in time when, in their intense sense of God's presence, God chooses to speak in His own terms and in His own way to man.

Out of this kind of secure commitment in darkness and in the unknown comes a special kind of knowledgeableness and wisdom that has always been associated with such mystics.

It is a wisdom not reduceable to human terms but, by definition, a wisdom *beyond*. Such contemplation brings a security which no human element or agent would have the capacity to give. The trust and commitment to God requires a person's having to trust himself in the mystery of darkness. But there is a security in the darkness. It acts as a protective filter from the brilliance of God. Therefore within the darkness, if one accepts and commits oneself to the witness of faith, is a wisdom which surpasses any conceivable human wisdom and one in which—in a friend to friend belief—we can trust. In this trusting faith is the security of Newman's "kindly light" that leads through the encircling gloom.

# VII. What Can Man Believe In?

IN answering the question, "What can man believe in?" one might begin simply by saying that he can believe in three things: himself, others, and God. To delineate the meaning, however, of such an answer involves us in a discussion first of all, of what we mean by "belief." How is faith different from a process of knowing or of reasoning or proving? The answer also involves us in defining *how* one believes in oneself, in others, and through the self and others, in God.

## FAITH AS UNCONDITIONAL COMMITMENT

We can begin then with what is meant by "belief." As a result of a common confusion, perhaps attributable to the religious biblical emphasis of the sixteenth century, the extenuation of printing, and the resultant influence of the written and printed word, belief has come to mean for many, the expression of some kind of creed or document, or perhaps a list of propositional or creedal statements because these in some measure structure the nature of belief.

Yet such a view of belief is, in itself, misleading. What we mean by belief is rather that which is both a prelude and a concomitant of hope and love as we explained in Chapter VI. Faith, in that sense, has to do with persons, rather than with verbal, creedal statements or documents.

156

Faith is seen as an abandonment and a commitment of the self. This has been expressed in a modern way as an "unconditional positive regard," both of the ego towards the self and of the ego-self towards others. For faith to be operational and real therefore, it must be positive and unconditional. One has no faith in another person if he is negative towards that person, nor does one have faith in another person if he sets up a series of restrictive conditions determining whether he trusts and hopes in the other person. Such restrictions, conditions, and negations vitiate at their inception the nature of a genuine personal commitment and a true faith and trust in the other.

What is said of a commitment towards others in unconditioned positive regard can also be said of the self. The ego must, in some very real way, have an unconditioned positive regard towards its own self. A man who gives in to negativism and hypothetical propositions towards himself is caught in his own masochistic death-wish instinct. Perhaps this helps to explain the constant recurrence of the notion of a positive self-attitude, such as Dr. Coué's famous "Day by day I am getting better," of fifty years ago, or the more recent "positive thinking" of Norman Vincent Peale, and the positive motivation concepts of W. Clement Stone. Simple as such an attitude may appear, it expresses the need for a conscious positive self-attitude. It gives a person a simple motivational formula, which aids him to hold a positive regard towards himself. This is the essence of faith in oneself. The confident man, believing in himself, is characterized by an unconditioned positive attitude towards himself.

## THE NEED FOR PROOF EXCLUDES LOVE

While propositional statements must be made, they are secondary to the personal "leap" that Kierkegaard made

157

famous. Such a commitment is necessary if there is to be any genuine hope and love of the self and others, and through others of God. We cannot approach ourselves negatively, hemmed in with a series of conditions around which we accept ourselves, nor can we approach others or God in that way. The mystics understood this in the recurrent theme of abandonment of the self to God. The most fundamental aspect of faith, therefore, is a commitment without restriction. It is in this way that one arrives at hope and, in a very special way, at love.

We can see the negative attitude implied in restrictions and conditions, or even in the excessive "reasonableness" of "proof" if we consider a typical scene from a modern play, television episode or movie. In any given scene the clues quickly indicate that the wife wants "proof" of where her husband was when he is two hours late for dinner, as well as exact evidence that he is telling the truth. From one point of view this could be called a "scientific" or "reasonable" attitude. The husband should be willing to offer proof of where he was and why he is late. Yet intuitively and without explanation the audience, even the least sophisticated among them, immediately senses that there is comparatively little love existing between them as a couple. If so much proof is demanded when any element of mystery or of the unknown occurs in their relationship, they cannot really trust or love one another.

Conversely, if the opening scene shows the wife dismissing the husband's being late as understandable and in no need of explanation, then the same audience quickly sees that a state of love exists between the couple. The more one demands reasons and explanations, the less the atmosphere of trust and love is conveyed. The more conditions that are set up which demand proof, the less will love be evident. On the contrary, love is revealed when open and simple acceptance occurs with no proof demanded. Love and its concomitant trust is a genuine positive affirmation in the face of the unknown and the mysterious.

## THE PARADOX OF BELIEF IN SELF

Faith is itself, therefore, an act of giving oneself to oneself, to others, and ultimately to God. The act of faith must proceed from a willingness both to possess the self and at the same time to give the self. Here we are in a strange paradox and popular language itself embodies something of it. We talk about "finding" oneself, "being" oneself, and "believing in oneself." How can I, if I am lost, find myself? And, who is lost and who is found? Or how can I, being myself, not believe in myself? How can I cut myself off from myself and not believe in myself?

What we are attempting to discuss is made difficult because language, as we have previously seen, while very rich in subtle if confused awarenesses, is also confusing in the various ways it phrases these observed divisions in the self. The place of the "ego," the "self," the "whole person" often gets mixed up in confused terminology. We say, for example, that a person is "going to pieces," and he should "take a hold of himself," and "pull himself together," and everyone knows or feels, in general and in feeling tone, what we mean. But what, precisely, does this mean? This we will attempt to discuss without, however, entirely resolving the confusion in these popular expressions.

The act of the ego making the self the object of its belief or disbelief, while it appears to be contradictory, is, at the same time, a human experience. Such an apparent paradox is possible. We know from personal awareness and experience of belief in the self that one can have confidence in

159

himself and so make far better use of himself by an abandonment of the ego to the self. Failure to do this negates and divides the self.

Prior to belief in oneself is the placing of value on the self. We have pointed out a person's dichotomous language which yet is understood by anyone hearing him, "I am disgusted with myself," or even "I hate myself." In this state where the ego is in a negative, resistant attitude towards the self, one can see that no genuine faith or trust in the self is possible. Insofar as one gives himself genuinely to himself, he does so first of all by valuing himself, by having a deep sense of his worth as a self. Prior to any gift of oneself to the self, or prior to any confidence or faith in oneself, there must be the statement, "I respect myself," "I have positive regard for myself," "I think myself to have genuine significance and worth." One must, in a word, assume a "redemptive" attitude towards himself in order to believe in himself. By "redemptive" we mean that one must convey worth and value on himself in order that he feels himself worthy to be the recipient of the gift of the "I" believing in the self. For if one believes a gift to be of no value, then its reception is valueless.

## THE NECESSITY OF COUNSEL WITH THE SELF

One might raise a further issue about the obvious dichotomy in the self which is contained in phrases like "one must possess the self," or "one hates oneself and one must love oneself." These segmented phrases of the self seem to leave the ego incomplete. One reason for a tendency to self-segmentation is inherited through our culture. Our culture has given us a Cartesian-Kantian idea of the psyche or the self, namely, one that is highly intellectual and fundamentally voluntarist. If we consider the Kantian

160

sense of duty, which primarily determined the will and the categorical imperative that directed it, we recognize that Kant, like Descartes, saw no place for the emotions, the instincts and the soma as related to the psyche and therefore, as part of the human person. The body was cut off and removed from the psyche and this separation justified the current mechanistic notions of the time in which both Kant and Descartes lived.

If we look now, however, at the unity of the self, we recognize that we are perhaps more comfortable with the Aristotelian notion of the psyche or the self as "informing" the soma and being its basic life principle. The acts of both knowing and willing in the self would seek to penetrate into the emotions, instincts, and soma. This involves the struggle to gain self-insight and greater integrated control of the self in much the manner that modern psychotherapy and counseling have worked out and described. The process of possessing the self, of loving the self, or of finding the self, would be one of taking counsel with the self. It would involve a penetrating into the significance and meaning behind the segmented urges of the emotions, instincts, and soma and a recognizing of the particular segmented purpose of each of these actions. In this way one would slowly bring them together into some kind of organismic wisdom. In a particular evaluation and decision, such wisdom would integrate what is best in the soma, emotions, and instincts in the direction of what seems, in terms of personal insight and past and present self-awareness to be best for the total integrated self.

Before faith in the self can really occur and, therefore, before hope and love in self can really occur, one must avoid, in Plato's term, the "tragedy of the unexamined life." One must undergo a constant taking counsel with the self in order that, in a particular experience, evaluation, or choice, he can take the best elements of his awareness of the self, somatically, emotionally and instinctively and coordinate them with what seems best to the intellectualized and voluntary aspects of the self. In this sense there is a kind of owning up to the self.

Usually in children and often in adults, there is an unwillingness to accept the body as being part of the self, as seen, for example, in the expression, "my feet are killing me." Here one seems to view parts of the body as being against the self. The same can be true of the instincts and the emotions. They can be seen as inimical to the self. In "owning up to the self" or the self possessing its total self, we have a self-insightful process which seeks the integrity of all aspects of the self—soma, instincts, emotions, intellect, and voluntary functions. In this process one believes in an integrated wisdom that with the soma, instincts, and emotions coordinated together in the best sense of self-realization, works together towards the good of the whole person. It is the kind of unconditioned positive belief in the self that the counseling-therapeutic process brings about when it is successful.

## COUNSEL: THE INFORMING OF THE SELF

There must be a period then, in which a person takes counsel with himself and in this process there is a kind of "informing," of the self. There is a real "informational" relation with the self, in the basic sense of *informing* the whole self or integrating it with the insightful awarenesses of the cognitive self as it strives to understand and penetrate and "in-form" the emotions, instincts, and soma.

In this sense we would be speaking about the notion of

"believing that I may understand." By this description of belief, we mean the positive regard one has towards the whole self. One respectfully approaches the soma, instincts, and emotions to seek the reasons that are mysteriously hidden in their apparently segmented motivation. By approaching them in this way one begins to understand then to integrate them with the awarenesses of the ego in the conscious intellectual and voluntarist aspects of the self.

The concept of "in-forming" or integrating the whole person is often difficult for us because, as we noted, our culture is still so caught up in a dichotomized inheritance from both the Cartesianism and Kantianism of an intellectual and voluntary process completely removed from the rather automatic mechanistic soma. Even now, while we use words that speak of a unified person, we are perhaps still culturally handicapped and impaired. This is because it is hard for us to feel a respectful regard for the soma, instincts, and emotions as having "reasons" that could be integrated and coordinated with the conscious cognitive will.

## THE SELF RELATED TO OTHERS

We might go into a further discussion of why "faith in the self," or total positive commitment to the whole person, is so difficult. We will do this by considering that aspect of the self which relates us to others and, in the capital sense, to the final Other, God. We are restating in another form a contention of Aristotle that friendly relations with others, or, in our terms, unconditional positive regard towards others, begin with a genuine friendship with the self. This positive regard or "faith in the self" initiates the subtle process of integration of the self, in contrast to the

163

dichotomized aspects of the self. This then makes possible the faith, hope, and love that emerge between the ego and the whole self. Through this process too, the integrated self can begin to give itself in faith to others and to trust, hope in, and love others. Consequently, the result of our relationship to others is rather predetermined by how we work out our relationship to ourselves. One must be a true friend to himself before he can be a friend to others. Somewhat like looking through dark glasses, our attitude towards ourselves colors our regard for and view of others.

Aquinas extends this notion further through the text so well known in Christian tradition, that one must "love one's neighbor as oneself," and then in and through love of neighbor and oneself, one must love God. He comments that the love of self is the model of which the love of neighbor is the copy and that the copy will only be as valid, sound, and operationally effective as the model. In other words, as we love or hate ourselves, so our relation to others will be one of love or hate. He suggests an insightful knowing that leads to the ego making a positive commitment to the whole integrated person.

## SELF-INSIGHT

What we mean by "insight" is not a kind of abstractive, gestaltist configuration on the mathematical model. We mean rather the painful struggle necessary in the mystery of the self in order to come up with those awarenesses, confused as they may be, that are filled with subtle meaning and significance to the self. "Insight" means the slow integration of particular somatic, instinctive, or emotional elements with the broader and more extensive

164

cognitive awarenesses of the self. Such insight into one's whole self is essential for the regard, respect, and love of the self. It would be creative with regard to the whole self, that is, it would bring about a new self. This has various parallels with the Christian birth of a new self, particularly in its Pauline emphasis and as we have seen in learning.

Carl Rogers has spoken of the fundamental reasonableness he finds in his clients when he genuinely strives to understand them. This would seem to imply that soma, instincts, and emotions have a basic reasonableness in what they do—a kind of "reason" for being and acting. Unfortunately, this reasonableness is narrow and restricted to the immediate somatic, instinctive, or emotional need—like the swelling of the nose in vasomotor rhinitis, or the defensive eye blink. It sometimes corresponds to the need of the whole person. Most often, however, it can impede or even frustrate the whole person's fulfillment. It is the whole self's struggle for "insight" into the self that pulls these conflicting, narrow reasons together and integrates them with the needs of the whole person.

In considering the issue of the self and why we must struggle for insight into the mystery of the whole self, one comes to a prior concept of some "disintegration" in man. Many traditions have attempted to explain the apparent division in the self by proposing that because of some primal fault or some fundamental error in the human condition, man has no longer the kind of integration that he might normally have had, or that he might be thought ideally to have. According to some traditions this disintegrated state is a less natural, in the sense of less ideal state of the human condition and so might be conceived of as a punishment. There are, however, other ways of looking at the same situation. These do not disregard the concept of disintegration but rather suggest other aspects that could help to extend and clarify it.

## THE ANXIETY OF EXISTENCE

Any discussion of the dichotomy, conflict, partitions, segmentations, or divisions within the self, tends to focus, as a result of influences from Kierkegaard through Freud to modern existentialism, on the "angst" of the human condition. Somehow man experiences from the first moment of existence a state of anxious concern and threat in regard to both his own existence and the meaning and ultimate value of that existence. However we explain this "angst" in man, it follows that it leaves him with a great fear of any kind of risk or any sort of engagement with the unknown.

In this sense the scriptural text that "perfect love casts out fear" would provide a sharper awareness of the dichotomy. What faith, hope, and love have to work against is a basic fear in man that causes him to shrivel up in his own ego and so renders him unwilling to trust or to give himself in any kind of openness, even to those other aspects of himself that would complete his integration. So the man who "hates himself," or is negative towards himself, is also a man who is afraid of himself, afraid to trust himself. The fear of the self, and fear to trust the self, will be radiated to others, and in a religious context, to the Supreme Other, and will result in the same kind of anxious unwillingness to commit oneself. This is basically the issue in the Parable of the Talents. While we popularly interpret the parable as an intellectualist search for talents and the obligation of the more talented one, the heart of the parable centers on a self-inverting, narcissistic fear

This fear caused the man with the one talent to bury it and not to risk, in anxiety of the master, any commitment of himself or the talent, but rather only to protect himself and hold on. Here, as in the text, "He that shall save his life shall lose it," such inverted anxious protection of the ego against a total commitment to the self and others, is the very opposite of that act which would "cast out fear" and move in the direction of love and, therefore, also of hope and faith.

We are speaking, then, of man's faith in himself, others and God and of his attempt to overcome the primal "angst" which seems to characterize the human condition. This demands confidence in oneself and the capacity to work against the primitive defense of the self and so to arrive at some kind of abandonment or going out that accompanies the gift of the self to others.

This is a struggle that is common to the human condition and not peculiar to any of us. It is a struggle against a narrowness and a closing-in on ourselves which would be the opposite of extending ourselves and so opening up to others. The fundamental "angst" of the human condition militates against man being able to go out and take the risk of giving himself to another person in love and also in faith. There is something self-defeating in this, as we observe in the Parable of the man who had the one talent. The thing that he needs most he has the least chance of getting. This is a characteristic result of the "angst" of the human condition. It cannot be described except as an almost blind fear, a fear of losing existence and the narrow and often self-defeating need to hang on to it. The drowning man's grabbing at the rescuer's throat may suggest something of this primitive, blind, self-defeating panic.

## INTEGRATION FROM CHANGE IN PERCEPTION

If we look more closely at the self-defeating fear or "angst" of commitment, we notice in the German word itself—which suggests being "cornered"—that such a condition is narrow and constrictive. This is revealed in the process of taking counsel with the self and gaining insight into the mysterious aspects of the self. If we look at the meaning of such "angst" or narrowed constriction in the self, we find that in the emotion of fear, in the instinct of defense, and in the primitive somatic reactions, we see that there is a kind of wisdom in the defensive fear and protectiveness that keeps the other out. The emotions respond to what appears to the organism as threatening. But we realize that by a broader insight-awareness, the threatening object can assume a totally different perceptual field. This change in perception can relax the fear, anxiety, and the instinctive defenses. At the same time the soma itself often responds with a relaxed biochemical and physical change.

One can see this illustrated by taking a person by surprise and waving one's hand in front of his eyes in the experiment we previously alluded to. The subject's first reaction, because he is responding simply to a threatening object at a primitive subcortical level, is to pull his head back, to blink and often to experience other primitive threat reactions, such as perspiration in the palms and increased heart beat. However, if one continues to do this for eight to ten waves of the hand, the subject indicates, often by a slight smile, a relaxed feeling of security. He no longer blinks but instead he openly trusts the experimenter.

In the experiment nothing is said. What happens is that the subject himself changes his perception of the field of

168

what is happening and broadens his awareness of the whole self, so that he is no longer threatened but recognizes that he is the object of an illustration in a simple experiment of defense reflex. Seeing the positive value in what he is doing, he is now somatically, instinctively, and emotionally integrated around his broader and more comprehensive cognitive awareness of the total situation.

In this simple illustration we see how the process of taking counsel with the self involves the ego's cognitive working through of the whole self and so bringing about a different perception. Consequently, the narrowed "angst"-segmented view that caused the instincts, soma, and emotions to have their own narrowed and segmented reaction gives way, through a total self-awareness, to a different gestalt, configuration, or conceptualization. This results in a changed response in the soma, instincts, and emotions which are now integrated through the ego's cognitive struggle to grasp the total situation. This corresponds to the process that brings about greater integrated insight into the mystery of the total self. While it is not the clear and distinct awareness that, according to a mathematical model, our scientific Cartesian culture might demand as prerequisite for a real conviction or proof, yet it has the cognitive ability to bring about a more integrated response of the whole self as a result of a changed and broader self-configuration. The cognitive aspects of the self somehow penetrate the soma, instincts, and emotions with a new view and so relieve them of their narrow defenses and cornered sense of "angst."

Handling the threat constructively by an integrated self would be the redeeming act. The ego gives value to the self through the realization that it will not hurt the self. In abandoning oneself in openness by not becoming defensive, as in the eye-blink experiment, the self is enhanced and redeemed. The self is now seen as a human person who controls cognitively the instincts, soma, and emotions and is no longer the victim of them. This is the same path, in a more complex way, that any process of counsel-integration must follow, whether by the person himself or with the aid of counseling.

## THE ORGANISM'S QUEST FOR DEATH

We might now explore how there might be purpose or meaning behind the human organism's resistance to trusting both the self and others. We are led here to Freud's conception, expressed in his *Beyond the Pleasure Principle*, of the notion of death-wish and death-instinct as being fundamental to man. As we pointed out in the chapter on "The Dynamics of Prayer," the organism recognizes the one irrevocable and certain truth about itself, namely, that it is going to die. It recognizes this from the moment of birth and so is always preparing itself for death. Looked at in this way there is a purposive intent in the organism by which it tries to maintain itself as close to death as possible throughout its life. If the goal of the organism is death, as it obviously is, then it is to the organism's basic advantage not to allow life forces to take too strong a hold lest it lead the organism falsely away from its more obvious goal. Too much commitment to life would seem to make it all the harder for the organism to accept and reconcile itself to death when that inevitable and predictable end is realized.

Seen from the primitive intent of preserving the organism for death as its direct end, one recognizes a narrow but profound validity to this kind of death-instinct. To be sure, if a man is to die, then it could appear safe that he stay close to the goal of death throughout his life. Contrary to this would be any urges to life which, by definition, would seem to be leading him away from admitting

170

his real immediate goal which is death. The life urges could even seem to lead to the most tragic of self-deceptions, namely, that one is going to live interminably and that he need not face or prepare himself for death.

One need only look at oneself to realize that consciously man does have an unwillingness to face the inevitable end of his organism. Consequently, he can tend to set himself up for this tragic self-deception. The counterbalance of the organism holding out for a death-instinct and a death-wish and always counteracting every life drive of the organism by the reminder of the necessity of its being willing to die offers great, if narrowed, wisdom to the human person. It also offers an understandable counterbalance to the euphoria of assuming that one will live forever, granting that others die. The death-instinct, as Freud called it, then, keeps man close to the end of the organism even when he is always trying to vault himself over that inevitable purpose and goal.

## THE OPTION FOR OPENNESS

In their narrowness—while they may fulfill a death-wish—the instincts, soma and emotions can also, for the same reason, deceive a person and trick him and cause him to be afraid to live—afraid of trusting himself and others. Such fear and mistrust can result in bitter rejection of the self. This, in turn, can lead away from integration and self-approval to self-disgust and even to a greater state of disintegration and escape. The character of Judas could symbolize this destructive aspect of the death-wish, in his unwillingness to forgive himself.

These same characteristics can be applied to the other. The other is capable of betrayal or of misusing one's trust. In our earlier illustration of the eye blink, for example, the experimenter could actually slap the subject; what the

171

person would feel after this, catches a fundamental human situation. One solution is expressed in the popular phrase, "Fool me once, shame on you, fool me twice, shame on me." But an alternative would be for the subject to trust the experimenter the third time. He would do so through a broad cognitive realization that the slap was an illustration of how the instincts and emotions are not always wrong, and, therefore, the slap was not an insult but, as before, simply an illustration for other's benefit. This would put him in a self-attitude that is dignified and redemptive, and not rejecting. He may then willingly trust and be open on the third trial, neither blinking nor pulling his head back. But if he feels that he has been shamed and humiliated and if he cannot see that he was in the same dignified position in the second trial as in the first, then he will remain the victim of his own defensive encapsulation. He will not only blink and throw his head back but probably throw his hands up in defense as well. Or he may refuse to participate further. He will not "turn the other cheek."

It is this third situation and option that seems to be the human condition. What does one do after one has been hurt? The text that we should "love our enemies" suggests that we must love that which first appears inimical to us, as the deceptive self may appear inimical to the ego when it is in a state of hatred or disgust towards itself. Similarly, another person may appear inimical to one when it seems to him that the other has betrayed and misused his faith. Yet everyone at some time experiences betrayal, or abuse. If the human condition is not to settle then for the path of "saving one's life" through a narrow protective death-wish and so losing the broader and more comprehensive meaning of life; if one is not simply to give up really living by staying as close to death as possible, living, so to speak, in a cemetery, then one takes this risk of repeatedly letting come forth all the life instincts that are in him. He does so in the realization that he could be betrayed, that he could be misused, that in a particular instance, this is possibly a situation "inimical" to him. Yet he still opens himself up in love, faith, and trust in the face of that possible option.

One either passively accepts threat and resigns to defensive death-withdrawal urges, or he struggles towards life, towards fuller being beyond. The very struggle to change the perception of what appears to be an inimical relationship is in itself a dignifying and life-centered act. Then going beyond that struggle would be the conscious commitment to the opening up of oneself. One may and usually does know that one could lose in the relationship. But it is the intentional, purposive act of opening oneself, even in the light of possible betrayal, that is uniquely *for* the other and *away from* protective narcissism.

For this act to be possible, as we have seen, it must flow out of the previous commitment and acceptance of oneself. The ego has in fact been deceived and betrayed many times in the past by the self and so it will tend not to want to take the risk. Yet this is precisely one aspect of the Christian message of loving what may seen "inimical," namely, that one does go out to what may appear to betray. This also characterizes the human condition—the ego has been betrayed by the self. Unless one can bring these two into some kind of trusting harmony within himself, he cannot go out in love to another, and particularly if the other happens at first to seem to be an "enemy."

## LIFE-OR-DEATH RESPONSE

Applied to others then, the life-death conflict explains many of the most painful and confusing as well as most

173

PSYCHOLOGICAL DYNAMICS IN RELIGIOUS LIVING

glorious and enhancing of human experiences. For in any human relationship the person must first trust himself and his life impulses enough to give himself over in some kind of insightful taking counsel with the self. The resultant cognitive integration then allows him to give a gift of his whole self. This, of course, is a different thing than talking about simply "loving" others in an intellectual sense. This is a gift of self-including emotions, instincts and soma— openly to another in an act of trust which is a prelude to, and necessary part of, an act of love.

In the process of this one's life impulses emerge. One might even say that, at first, these emergent life impulses can startle the other person, much as the hand suddenly waved before the eyes startles the other person, causing spontaneous defense, negation, and arousal of the death-instinct. Because this negative response from the other person is unexpected and even illogical, it is one of the most difficult of human experiences to accept. Stated another way, it is understandable that when a person has struggled to bring to life some commitment between his ego and his self, and has succeeded in expressing the results of this struggle to another person or to a group, he can, in fact, logically expect their redemptive understanding and sharing. He might logically expect a sharing of his life-impulses and of his integrated cognitions and deep and even painful self-investments. That is, the person can normally expect what might be called an incarnate-redemptive response on the part of others in which they open themselves up emotionally, instinctively, somatically, and cognitively to a genuine effort to what he is trying to communicate.

In fact, however, we know from repeated personal experience in this kind of situation that such a response seems only rarely to occur. It most often occurs only when

174

one has made his personal revelation to skilled therapists and counselors because they themselves have undergone a long and rigorous training. The result of their training enables them to control their self-oriented impulses and truly to "understand." These people, by virtue of their skill and self-control, are able to give the kind of understanding integrative response that seems so profoundly helpful and gives such a sense of worth and redemptive value to the other person.

Why such a skill and art is necessary, is evident in the process that the training of people in skilled counseling and psychotherapy reveals. Apparently the first impulse that is aroused in another when a person tries to express some kind of life expression about himself, is an expression of one's own death-urges. These will segment, distort and divide what the person has said. "He didn't understand. He cut me to pieces," he may say afterwards as he painfully relates to others what happened to him. He is describing a divided and segmented feeling that he was not understood but that he was fragmented. In trying to communicate himself, he in fact came away wounded, perhaps almost wounded to death. It will then be very difficult for him to have sufficient trust and hope ever again to struggle to project his personal life urges out to anyone else.

This is the description that the client often gives of himself in the beginning stages of counseling or psychotherapy. If a person is talking about a relationship in marriage, it is often a painful one of how he has tried to communicate with his wife, or she with her husband, and death effects have followed to the point where he or she has become protectively encrusted and unwilling ever to trust again. The same thing may happen with children in relation to parents, or parents to children. It can happen to

175

groups of people living or working together. The end effect has been that when one struggled to express some aspect of life, some elements of hope and value and meaning that were of deep significance to himself, he met with death. The negative, destructive, segmented, divisive responses of others left him nearly dead. In his wounded condition he understandably comes to the therapist for some kind of skilled healing or therapy. Rather than responding with understanding, most people react to another's deep revelation and commitment with responses that are divisive and segmented because such open statements are a threat in that they represent a life-force. The negative response is an attempt to segment whatever integration the person has acquired and so reduce him to the same condition as the one responding.

Therefore, a person who attempts to communicate any creative aspects of himself has often to seek out someone who is skilled in understanding and listening to him, if he is not to stir up death-urges. He would have to go to others who have overcome their own death-impulses even if only enough to listen to him and hear him out. This alone helps. But it takes more, as we saw, to further his creativity. However, when such creative understanding occurs then the person leaves healed and feeling genuinely fulfilled as a result of such communication. This sensitive understanding, like a successful trapeze act, leaves the one who took the leap positively and constructively encouraged to continue the creative thinking process and in expressing himself to be able to hope for and trust in the continuation of such redemptive communication.

## A MODEL OF COMMUNICATION

What the skilled counseling therapist does, out of learned self-control and self-possession demonstrated by his deli-

176

cate holding to cognitive-feeling life responses, could be the model for what we must all struggle to do with one another in any kind of creative communication. This could be the model of any kind of effort at communication and community. One person would struggle cognitively and personally to preserve life by holding himself open to the other and to the mysterious struggle for what is valuable and sound in the other's effort to understand himself and to take counsel with himself or to communicate some plan, project, or series of ideas. He would be able, in a life giving atmosphere, to present himself without defenses. He could confidently expect understanding and the con-validation of the worth of his communication. This "consensual validation," to use Harry Stack Sullivan's term, or convalidation, would carry with it the confirmation of his value as a person—in his own uniqueness. In a word, such convalidation would be "redemptive."

## THE OTHER

Until now, while we have considered belief in the other, it has been related to the self and self-needs. We have primarily interrelated the conflict of the ego in its moving out from "angst" and death to trust the self. This demands some elements of integration which relate soma, instincts and emotions to the broader aspects of the self. This process also involves moving out to the other. There is, however, one special element which an encounter with the other offers the self. There is something unique in the other, as other, which the self cannot give to itself. Only through the other can the limits of the self be defined and gradually recognized.

Childhood begins not only in "angst" but also in a narcissistic inversion and self-preservation. The developmental process is a slow and sometimes painful restricting

177

of the self in the process of going out to the other. A person defines the limits of himself as he comes into conflict with the limits of the other. One sees that there is, in the experience of the other, a kind of a limiting of the self's will.

## INTERNALIZATION OF WILL TO POWER

Alfred Adler's concept of the "will to power," as being in conflict with "will to community," expresses this well. Not only is the self caught up in narcissistic inversion in early childhood, but its need for identification and meaning comes from a sense of power which others first convey on the self. Then the self gradually conveys this to the self. The will to power flows at first from the child's struggle for independent self-affirmation and self-identity. The early process of consensual validation, or convalidation from the other, consists primarily in attributing to the small and growing child his awareness of and confidence in his own independent power over many conditions around him. Independence itself involves the dignity that goes with one's own self-identity and one's right to guiltless expression of one's will, in certain conditions. Having one's will dignifiedly recognized by the other's approval and acquiescence is itself a positive convalidation of the will to power.

One might therefore propose that the first redemptive state in the child occurs as his will to power is validated and internalized. Increasingly, his sense of identity and self-worth is in some measure determined by the degree to which this power is recognized by others as coming from him and having its own rights in him. In the struggle, for example, over the fetish object that many children undergo, a struggle sometimes expressed too in their anxieties over nightmare fears, one often sees this. No matter

178

how the therapy proceeds, it reveals a gradual internalizing of the child's power over the fearful object. The child begins to assert himself as being more powerful than the fearful object. The power of this security-giving or fearful object—be it doll or horrendous nightmare image, is in some manner the creation of the child himself. He grows to understand that he has given the power to the fetish to give him security or the nightmare to scare him. He can then take it away and so be independent and freed.

## THE SACRIFICE OF SELF-ASSERTION

Power, as a means to worth, dignity, redemption, and self-identity, is very basic to a person's sense of value and his own sense of worth. This must therefore be conveyed to the child, and repeatedly convalidated by those around him, so that he grows sure and confident in his own power, his own worth and identity. It is in and through the sense of power that his sense of worth grows.

There is, however, another phase which seems to be the exact opposite of this. It is usually expressed in the fear that the child may become too superior in his pursuit of power and self-excellence. This can happen and can result in a tendency to "run over" others and to use them. Sometimes in the manipulation of others there may be the appearance of caring for them but only as a deception. The real intent is what others can do for the person himself. Such manipulation, control, and maneuvering of others can assume the self-deceptive disguise fundamental to narcissism. Narcissus, in love with his own image in the pool, never knew that the image was that of another, and so when it disappeared as he tried to embrace it, he felt cursed by the gods.

One of the deceptive aspects of apparent giving of the self, and having faith and trust in others, is that it could

179

finally be a self-centered maneuver. In fact one has never really given oneself to the others at all. He has always given himself only in those aspects which further represent and enhance himself through the other. This, indeed, would be a Sartrean world of "no exit" from the captivity of the self.

In any kind of community relationship, in marriage, and in a special way in group counseling or psychotherapy, the boundary lines between selves begin to emerge and assert themselves. Wills to power clash and as they clash they also define limits of individual selves. It is here that some kind of gift of the self is required. For a going-out to the other to occur, one must first possess himself and so have a strong sense of his own identity, power and worth. One sacrifices this self-power in giving himself openly to the other.

As Adler suggested, will to community, in the sense of genuine communion and communication with the other, does involve the giving up of the power of the self. The urge to hold on to self-power might come from that aspect of the self that holds us close to death. In giving up of the power of self-affirmation, one gives up too the possible self-aggrandizement that this may represent. But when one has given up this power, he trusts that a greater enlarging of the self will occur. But this occurs in and through the other, once the abandonment to communion and union with the other has been made.

Prior then to any gift of the self, or belief in, hope, and love of the other, must be the ancient awareness of "to each his own." This includes both the recognition of one's own limits and of the place where the frontier and dimensions of the other begin. When one has clearly separated himself from the other, he can then give himself to the other as distinct from a narcissistic projection of

180

himself on the other in self-deception. One must be ready to allow the other to function independently in his own self-assertion within the boundaries of his own self-dimension. The other is then seen as a person uniquely different from him and uniquely beyond him. Precisely because of both this unique difference and the unique "beyondness" of the other, a person must genuinely "leap" out of himself to reach that other.

The relationship of the ego to the self then cannot provide the self-limits which one's relationship to another demands. When two people for example, have internalized the will to power in themselves and have had it sufficiently convalidated, the will to power can give way to will to community. Communication between them is then possible. But one must give up the will to power in behalf of the other before community and communion can take place. They could, conversely, do this for another—each giving up his own self-affirmation as he recognizes the other's prior need to be understood and affirmed.

## THE NEED TO LOVE THE OTHER FIRST

In order then for two wills to power, facing one another, to come to some communion, resolution and realization, one must give over to the other. To prevent a death-rejection confrontation and static state, one of them must love first. By loving first we mean that one must openly foreswear his need for self-assertion and open himself up to be "used" by the other. In the model of counseling and therapy, it is the counselor or therapist who first wills to open himself up to be used by the other; he makes a love relationship possible by openly loving first. In a theological context, we noted what St. John says, "It is not that we first loved God but God first loved us." This suggests the necessity of one person giving himself first in

181

order that the other may feel convalidation. This gives him worth and validity. When he has arrived at a conviction of his valid self-identity he then can begin to open himself up to being a kind of instrumentality for another. The will to community can then operate in their relationship together. This comes from a conscious choice towards community and away from power by one in order that the other may be convalidated and grow in his own identity, self-affirmation and worth.

When two people are experiencing the limits of one another, one or both necessarily has to give into the will to community in order that the relationship remains one of communion and communication. This kind of conscious, willful giving up of the self to the other can perpetuate itself. One can learn to do this, and will to do it, for another. This would keep alive, constructive, and creative a threefold personal fulfillment in communication, communion, and community.

## RELIGION AS A BOND

A final concept would be contained in the word "religion." By "religion" here we mean, first of all, its common literal interpretation as being related to the idea of a bind, or bond. Any genuine relationship with the other is, in this sense, religious because it binds two or more people. As we have said, one can manipulate and maneuver the other for oneself narcissistically, and one can even go so far as to suppress any confused self-awareness that one is doing this. One can consciously deceive himself into thinking that he is genuinely concerned for, has faith in and is going out to the other when, in fact, he has never left the safe protection of the trapeze swing. He is only enticing and maneuvering the other to

182

trust him, but he will manipulate and control him as he pleases.

To break into this protective bind one must establish, by way of a faith commitment and abandonment, a different kind of bind or bond. This is a communion with the other which is open, unprotective, and expressive of life. The opposite is a closed and protective death-wish of self-inversion and narcissistic encapsulation. This kind of bind has to be willed. It is free because the opposite is always possible. Such a concept of "religion" then, is both free and an act of hope and love, as well as an act of faith. Were it not in some measure a genuine option then it has no meaning as a true commitment.

## ABANDONMENT TO A TOTAL OTHER

Applying this concept of "religion" to others, then, it constitutes a bind or bond freely willed. In a very special sense, however, this concept of religion is, as generally understood, particularly applicable to that Other which is unique and for whom we use the name, God. A person's approach to the Other, who is God, can take a variety of forms. He may, in the classical, reasonable *Preambula Fidei*, propose to himself that behind many of the confusions and conflicts of nature there is yet an orderliness and design. This implies a kind of force that is intelligent and that determines life and life's purpose and so leads one to the recognition of the existence of God. From such a recognition one can then make the same kind of commitment and bond that he makes towards another. But the conditions of this bond are that he is binding himself to the Other, usually according to one of the various traditional meanings that we attribute to the word "God."

Alternately a person can arrive at a need for and

183

commitment to God through an awareness of his own restlessness and the inadequacy of all possible life goals. This would be an intuition of the Other in a basic Augustinian sense. That is, one's whole being cries out in restlessness for some kind of total fulfillment and projection. A person can simply accept and admit the existence of such a Being and abandon himself. The experience of the friendship and love of that Being would follow from a kind of mystical awareness of prayer and divine communication, as we have already discussed.

However one does this, and by whatever creedal codes and delineations, whether Judaeo or Christian or otherwise, he binds and encapsulates himself through his faith commitment. One has bound himself in a commitment similar to his faith commitment both to himself and to others. But he has now committed himself in a very special way to that Being behind all beings, that unknown God. This is a relationship with the most mysterious of all the mysterious unfathomable mysteries of life. It can therefore represent the most total and most complete gift of oneself that is possible. One might see the religious bind to God as the ultimate fulfillment and zenith of all abandonments that one makes of oneself to others. Insofar as one abandons himself to another human being, there is always some kind of reflection of himself in that being, offering him some kind of narcissistic reassurance. He can say this is a being who has existence similar to his own. While all religions in a special way have some anthropomorphic elements in their image of God, the Judaeo and Christian religions have a highly personalized God. They have given us a belief in a God who is deeply sharing of the human condition and deeply understanding of all aspects of man. Yet even here the nature of the abandonment to God, as God, is totally beyond any image in man.

## THE UNCONDITIONED COMMITMENT

One might then propose that Religion, in the capital sense of that word as applied to God, is a very special bond of the self to the Other. It must, at its final level, be a total kind of faith in mystery because, by definition, the abandonment to this Other is Another totally beyond man. While, in most religious traditions the God-figure has, in some form, become incarnate or at least communicated with man in a human way, yet the human communication itself is only God's means of loving man and opening himself up to man's needs and limits. By definition God, in his own being, is a totally non-narcissistic object of man's faith, hope and love. This is why one must make a complete act of faith in God, despite whatever rational evidences and proofs may lead one to some kind of conviction of the existence and significance of God. In the act of faith one must abandon himself to another totally beyond the self and others. This is the unique quality of a Religious bond.

Any notion of faith then contains the word "bond" and so is closely associated with religion. A person who has in some way freely bound himself to another has made an act of faith and, therefore, in a general sense, could be considered a "religious" person. But in the formal Religious sense, the ultimate act of faith entails a bond to that which is most mysterious and unknowable. One has the most to lose in establishing a bond with this kind of Being. Consequently the risk of self and the faith-commitment involved are the greatest possible—greater than a belief in and commitment to any other person. If the risk of love is the norm of man's highest humanity, then in a certain sense, the love of God would be the most effulgent expression of this humanity. This is the most complete act of faith that one can make because it is the ultimate risk

185

and ultimate bond. In this context one might even say that the extent to which one can relate non-narcissistically to others could determine the extent to which he can relate to and establish this bond with the Ultimate Other.

## MAN: BOTH BEING AND BECOMING

To sum up then, we have proposed that man can have faith in himself, in others, and in God. We have defined faith by saying that while secondarily it involves creedal statements and propositions, it is primarily the expression of a man's own life force as he moves out of himself in openness to others. But he does this, first of all, by being open to all aspects of himself, particularly the mysterious areas of his somatic, instinctive, and emotional world. In trusting himself to these, he grows to see that even in their narrowed and segmented aspects, there is some purposive meaning.

By cognitive persuasiveness, man brings an integrated awareness in his action around an insightful taking counsel with himself. The resultant self-decision then secures the integrated cooperation of his whole psychosomatic person. He does this first with himself. As a result of the life-forces which emerge, he then opens himself up to communication with and genuine faith in and trust of others.

Through conscious control of his own will to power, a man can openly abandon himself to others' use of him, either according to the model of the skilled counselor or teacher, or in the personal communion and community sense of a faith, hope, and love engagement with others. Out of the bonds between himself and others and between the ego and the somatic, instinctive, and emotive aspects of the self, the most fundamental bond or commitment of all, that of profound Religious faith, can emerge. This is the leap to and the abandonment of oneself in a life experience in believing in, hoping in, and striving to love and so commune with the Divine Being whom we call God.

We have proposed that the same elements enter into all three commitments. The difference, we submit, is that they mount in the degree to which they demand a total abandonment of the self. One abandons oneself first to one's whole self, rather than merely to the immediately conscious aspects of the self. One then limits oneself in recognizing the limits of the other who, in large measure, reflects and resembles the self. A third kind of possible commitment is that to a total Other whom we call God and who is totally beyond the self. By its nature this demands the most complete faith and commitment of ourselves. We have proposed that in answer to the question "What can man believe in?"—man can believe in all three and, in proportion as he acts out, integrates, and commits himself to the life forces of this belief, he can know and experience a life beyond himself. This can also be a faith involvement in a life beyond the death encapsulation that is the most evident goal that he sees.

Freud, in discussing his concept of "beyond the pleasure principle," was delighted when Jones suggested to him that a good translation of his German term *"Jenseits"* would be "hereafter." Freud was pleased by this word because he heard it freshly, as people often do in a language they do not know well. He saw it not as a "here," followed by an "after," but as a word which is simultaneously "here," fusing into "after." If we look carefully, the word "beyond" also expresses this because it is being that is moving towards the "yonder." Stated in this sense, we would propose that what man can believe in is not only his humanity in a static sense, but his humanity

187

becoming beyond. In the combination of the "here" fusing into the "after," he is simultaneously "be-ing," "be-coming," "be-yond," as he fuses from the "here" into the "after."

An ancient Greek idea of the human transient condition was that of an arrow flying through the air. At no point is it "here." When one tries to locate it at a given point, it is already "after" and moving further into the "after" and "beyond." Something of this image catches man as he moves from the ego towards the integrated self and then out to others, and from this, out to God. This is the human being in the here-after that man can believe in.

One can say then that the basis of all faith is contained in the bond between the ego and the self. The same elements that are there are also between the self and others, and between the self and God. This represents a process of constant moving out of the ego and the self towards the beyond. This could be expressed in the definition of man as a "being-becoming-beyond." Man starts with the relationship of the ego to the self and moves to commitment to others and to God.

But a person does not have to do any of these things. One never has to leave the ego; he can stay in a narcissistic "womb" as long as he chooses and he never has to go out to the other, nor does he need to go beyond the other to any final Other. These things are in one's power to do or not to do. A basic dynamic then is the element of freedom that marks belief. A person is not forced into making this kind of bond or commitment, but if he does make the commitment then he can experience a greater integration of himself, and an enlargening of himself as he goes out to others and through others to God. This gift of the self to God would be made in the faith conviction that this experience would go beyond death into life.

It may seem strange but, for the human condition, it is faith and trust in the unknown in oneself and others, rather than the predictable, the studied-out, the carefully analyzed that leads to the really fulfilling human experiences. The carefully "figured-out" situation is often characteristic of the purely self-protective; whereas it is the mysterious, the unknown and the unclear that seems to provide the opportunity for this leap, the trapeze-like letting oneself go in a faith commitment to others and, in a religious sense, to a final Other. This is our meaning when we say that a man can believe in himself, others, and God.

# VIII. Being a Friend to Oneself

THROUGH personal experience, through folklore expressions, as well as through recent popular publications, we
are continually being made aware of the inner conflict that
seems always to exist within the self. The solution to this
conflict is in the direction of integration. Such integration
invokes coordination of various aspects of the self through
some kind of central awareness and control.

## THE DIVIDED SELF

There is, of course nothing new in man's awareness of his
inner conflict. Horace among the Latin poets understood
this well and talked about wishing and approving of the
good aspects of himself but nevertheless following elements of evil. St. Paul sharpens the same conflict by
talking about his own approval of what he wants to do and
desiring it, and yet finding himself caught up in following
the opposite. He is reiterating the theme of "a law of his
members" working against "the higher law," as he sees it,
of his spirit. Shakespeare summarized this universal conflict by, "If to do were as easy as to know what were good
to do, then chapels had been churches and poor mens'
cottages princes' palaces."

These and other similar expressions suggest a clear
awareness, through many centuries of tradition, of inner
conflict and division in the self. Man's disunified state is

190

seen in many folklore expressions that have become commonplace. Yet they contain a deep wisdom which represents a struggle to catch something common to us all. We are all somehow torn or at odds, or in conflict with ourselves.

## THE SOLUTION

Just as the awareness of inner conflict is not new, so neither is the awareness of a need for some kind of solution. Even the simple folklore realization that "I must pull myself together" is itself a subtle groping for ways to arrive at an integration of the divided self. Many other such expressions suggest an awareness that a solution lies in an inner-directed control and integration of the self. At a more intellectual level too, many solutions have likewise been proposed, ranging from the most recently sophisticated psychological and psychiatric awarenesses back to Greek drama.

Since such a wide variety of propositions and solutions exist, we have chosen to concentrate on one central theme. But this theme, in large measure, contains most of the core ideas and goals of other solutions. Our treatment will focus on a theme expressed by Aristotle, repeated by Aquinas, and related to the Judeo-Christian tradition. It is the notion that a man must truly be a friend to himself. He must have the same deep affection, regard, respect, and honor towards himself as he has towards others. Going even further, both Aristotle and Aquinas suggest a relationship similar to the self-concept theory of modern psychology. Insofar as one is a friend to himself, he sets up the model of how he can be a friend to others; and insofar as one is inimical to himself, and in this sense distorted in his view of an understanding of himself, he can victimize himself in the way he relates to others.

191

## LOVE AS MOTIVE

Aquinas, spelling out this concept from Aristotle, proposes that, following the Christian norm, one must love others as one loves oneself and that this relates in turn to one's love of God. But, says Aquinas, the love of self is the model that predetermines our relationship to others insofar as our relationship to others is copied from this model. The success of an artist who uses as his model another artist's painting, for example, will be predetermined to a large extent by the quality of the model. So if we take this view of Aquinas, the heart of Christian concern begins fundamentally with the way one loves oneself and the complex and subtle alternate ways that a person can knowingly, and even more frequently unknowingly, hate and so have a very unloving relationship with himself.

Aquinas makes the further point that since all our motivation in some way is determined by what we love, then in a certain sense we never do anything without loving what we do. We always do a thing out of some kind of loving desire related to what we see as a good for ourselves in some way. He deals with the question of the divided self and how it can operate by focusing on a paradox. The paradox is that we act out of love even when we hate ourselves, but we do so because we actually love to hate ourselves. The process here then is one of moving from loving-the-self-hating, to loving-the-self-loving. This catches a complicated, double kind of loving which can paradoxically be a loving-to-love or a loving-to-hate.

Applied first of all to the self, this kind of loving-to-love or loving-to-hate oneself, also extends out to others. We are, from this view, always motivated by love but we can, in fact, love to hate as well as love to love. Whatever a

192

person does he does in relation to some kind of model. There are two models that one can use: Everyone acts out of some kind of love but a person can either "love to hate" or "love to love," and if the model of his action is "love to hate" then that will be carried over to his relationships with others. But if one "loves to love," then that would be the model of his personal commitment to himself and the model for his relationship to others.

## THE ESSENCE OF FRIENDSHIP

Carrying this notion still further, Aquinas speaks of certain concepts that follow from the relationship of friends to friends. He states them on the basis that one should be a genuine and true friend to oneself. Hence he says that a friend likes the company of a friend and enjoys a certain openness and ease in the company of a friend. In the same way one should like the company of oneself and have an open and trustful relationship with the self. Friends also have confidence in one another and have an "unconditioned positive regard" towards one another because the essence of their friendship is constituted by open and genuine trust. These same conditions must act within the self. In a very real sense, the self trusts all other aspects of the person, as a person trusts his friend. In no sense, then, is one afraid of any aspects of himself, because this would mitigate against being a friend to himself. Obviously one is not in a friendship relationship with anyone towards whom one feels inimical or towards whom he feels threatened and anxious. There are, therefore, no aspects of the self that one is afraid of, or made anxious by, and as a friend to a friend, one trusts all phases of himself with an open, positive and confident regard.

Here, too, one might make an application of the

concept that one should love one's enemies. Such a positive regard towards aspects of the self that seem threatening and "inimical" will carry one through the first stages of anxiety and fear that one has towards himself. As long as such anxieties about oneself perdure one is not loving that which seems inimical, threatening, or fearful. The solution is to change one's perception of these aspects as inimical and so reorganize his approach to himself. He then sees these aspects in the light of something not threatening to him, but as something of value even if limited in what they respond to. He can then begin to genuinely trust and be secure in understanding these limitations. Just as one might move away from seeing others as inimical so a person moves away from seeing aspects of himself as inimical. Instead of being threatened by himself, he moves towards a positive response to himself. Fundamentally, it is necessary for one to move openly, in a non-defensive way, in a positive reaction to these inimical aspects of himself, so that he may see them as limited in their view yet loyal and, in some measure, *for* his welfare, rather than being seen as threatening and inimical. Hence one's hostile attitude towards himself is overcome by changing his conceptalization of these attitudes so that they are seen as something positive in relation to himself.

On the negative side, a kind of stagnation of the self can follow from a masochistic disregard and disrespect for the self. This produces a self-attack in which one is actually loving his own self-degradation and failure. This is a kind of death-wish in which one loves to see himself humiliated, as he would love to see any enemy humiliated. In a complicated and subtle way such a person is delighted at his own sadness, failure, and misery. Consciously or unconsciously, one sees himself as inimical and so in-

194

evitably wants to defeat himself. He can then enjoy the victory over his enemy which is, in this case, himself.

But, according to the positive self-model of how one relates to a friend, one can see that, contrary to any distrust of self, there is a trust and peacefulness with all phases of oneself. This would be similar to the trust and security that comes out of the repeated shared acts and situations that constitute friendship. One does not immediately become friends with another person or group of persons. Friendship is formed first by an open risk on the part of one or both, and the gradual consistent validation of this risk by a genuine, competent response on the part of the other person. Only through repeated convalidation of one's risk with another person will friendship slowly emerge. One might say that all relationships with others begin in a somewhat threatening, anxiety-ridden type of perception that could be described as "inimical." But by openly trusting and giving oneself to what appears to be an inimical situation, one slowly enables it to become, not a relationship of threat, but the relationship of friends.

## GROWTH OF FRIENDSHIP

Applied then to the self in its relationship to various aspects of the whole person, the same consequences would seem to follow. One conceivably initiates any relationship with one's emotions, instincts, and primitive physiological urges. These aspects of the self are experienced as initially threatening and therefore initially inimical. As a result, the first impulse is to be thrown into a defensive, protective reaction against such threat.

But if, on the contrary, a person pursues the same process with these aspects of the self that one pursues in the making of friends, then he controls and resists this primitive threat and inimical feeling. He rather cultivates

195

an open trusting of those aspects of the self that at first seemed threatening. They then can grow—as friends do—to become not only non-threatening but positively constructive and cooperatively helpful. In this sense then, one would proceed away from the threatening, inimical, primitive first impulsive reactions of the self as one would proceed away from the beginning negations and anxieties one feels towards unknown people. Just as this can lead to a confident trust, regard, respect and love which slowly emerges with others, so also this can emerge in relation to phases and aspects of the self.

Basic to any real regard for another person, and therefore basic to any friendship, is the necessity of rendering to him what is truly his own. This embodies the idea of justice. That is, one must fairly recognize both the strengths and weaknesses of the other person, the limits of his being, both positively and negatively. In so doing, one neither demands more of the other than he is genuinely capable of, resulting in a final sense of self-delusion; nor does one demand less of him, resulting in disrespect Rather, friendship demands a truthful engagement between friends so that the friend is truly known for what he both is and is not. He is recognized, understood, trusted, and fulfilled under the conditions of what he genuinely is and what he genuinely can do. He is neither mistrusted in ways in which he should be trusted, nor is he forced into false functions or tasks for which he is incapable. Such misinterpretation is a misuse of a friend. It misleads both the friend and the person, and in the end disillusions, disappoints, and defeats both. This is caused by the other person who has falsely placed confidence in him through an inappropriate and inadequate evaluation of his abilities and capacities.

196

## JUSTICE TO THE SELF

This same notion applies to a truthful understanding of what each aspect of the self can contribute. This requires a sensitive and perceptive process of growing to know and appreciate each aspect of the self. In order for one truly to be a friend to himself, he must know what he can expect from the various physiological, instinctive, emotional functions of the self. A kind of justice towards all aspects of the self is necessary if friendship with one's self elements is to be possible. In this regard a person would not attribute to them a kind of wisdom, refinement, sensitivity, or perception which they do not have. Nor would he mistrust them in those aspects where, through careful study and evaluation, such functionalities of the self have proved reliable and worthy of confidence and trust.

This phase of the friendship model of the self would explain the ancient conception that there must be, first of all, a profound knowing of the self. But as we see here, this knowing of the self would be similar to the gradual process and engagement by which a group of persons become friends. Working together in a common task, business, or sport, they grow to understand both their strengths and weaknesses.

They rely on, trust, and have confidence in these strengths, and do not misappropriate and misuse people where they are weak or inadequate. In this way a constructive process comes about. The strengths of one often offset the weaknesses of the other. Together they are far stronger in a unified, goal-directed, integrated way than each could be alone.

The integration of a person with himself would come

197

about in much the same manner. It begins with the observation and study of himself in the wide variety of tasks and situations in which he finds himself. In proportion as he understands his strengths, he comes to a cooperative and coordinated control of himself. All aspects of the self increasingly integrate around his knowledge of what each can contribute wisely to any given task or engagement. But he also recognizes weaknesses coming from narrow perceptions and inadequate or limited abilities and responses. The whole person then recognizes those ways in which the individual emotional, instinctive or somatic aspects of the self do not see as far or as broadly and therefore do not respond with the same total integration as certain basic intellectual and reasoning functions of the self. They can, therefore, be trusted only within the reasonable limits of what they can do.

Consequently, the mature coordination that would follow from the model of a group of friends working together, would need to exist in the self. There needs to be refined recognition of when particular responses of the self lead wisely. In this sense, the same kind of sensitivity that goes into the evaluation of what a group of friends can contribute to one another, is also needed in the individual's relationship to himself. That same evaluation, therefore, would go into the evaluation of all aspects of the self. This would require a refined and respectful trust of those emotional, instinctive, and somatic aspects of the self that could lead the self wisely as it reacts to a particular situation. But this would also modulate and restrain the whole self from trusting to the narrow reactions of some elements when such reactions would fundamentally mislead the self.

In this, however, the whole self, understanding all its personal circumstances, would be open rather than closed to all aspects and elements of the self. The right use of all aspects of the self would follow from a discriminated knowledge as one would grow to know a group of friends working together in a difficult series of tasks. Knowledge of the strengths of all elements of the self, even the most primitive would, at the same time, recognize the limitations of each element. This would prevent the defeat and disillusionment that follows when certain aspects of the self are followed unwisely.

## THE REFLECTIVE SELF

Looking again at this divided aspect, we see the self's capacity for reflection upon itself and its actions and processes. The self is capable of observing and analyzing what it has in fact done. This often leads to the kind of divisive and dichotomized statements that we mentioned earlier. When a person says, "I am disgusted with myself," he is saying something both meaningful and mysterious. It is meaningful because we all know the experience and the feeling. It is mysterious because it raises the question of how one aspect of the self, the "I," is able to feel an emotional disgust for another aspect of the operational self. The same question is raised when "I" feels positive towards the self, as in "I am very pleased with myself."

This double aspect of the self enters into every awareness, positively or negatively, whenever the self reflects upon itself. It is somewhat like two persons responding positively or negatively to one another. If they are negative, they may only slowly grow to grasp the reasons that produce this negative reaction between them. They may then gradually come to a positive appreciation of one another.

The self's pursuit of reflective self-understanding then,

is a taking counsel with the self. This might be seen in marriage counseling where two persons are deeply engaged and committed to one another in common life situations and tasks. As they penetrate negative resistances and hostilities to one another, they begin to see reasons for their actions that they could not see before. Gradually they become more positively orientated and more truly perceptive of themselves and one another. They then can cooperate better together.

Consequently, in discussing the self taking counsel with the self we are not simply operating on a model of individual counseling. We are also thinking according to the model of marriage and group counseling. According to the group model, the self relates to other aspects of itself at first negatively and then positively. A person thus encounters within himself similar kinds of defeats, misunderstandings, disillusionments, pains, and sufferings which, as husband and wife or as a group of people functioning together, people inflict on one another. He only slowly comes to disentangle these conflicts and to begin to see positive elements and meanings. In other words, the movement from "I am disgusted with myself to "I am pleased with myself" is similar to the movement— in group counseling—from "I am disgusted with them" to "I am pleased with them." The final result of positive relationships within the various aspects of the self seems like a description of the complicated process that taking counsel with the self in a relationship of friend to friends seems to involve.

Thinking about oneself in order to understand oneself is therefore more complicated than at first appears. One grows to see that the genuine integration of the self gives rise to a myriad of factors resembling the complexities of a

200

group of people deeply invested in one another. They only slowly grasp how they might facilitate the best use of themselves and one another. So, a person only slowly grows to appreciate positive elements in his emotional instinctive and somatic levels, that rightly understood and facilitated, can be of great value to his whole person. This slow acquisition of appreciation, understanding and use of various aspects of the self is like the way a group counseling process facilitates a group regard for one another and more adequate cooperation together.

## COUNSEL WITH THE SELF

We can now consider how one takes counsel with oneself in this complex way that we have suggested. Such counseling with the self, of course, can be done and most often must be done, alone. It can, however, also be done in and through another person. In our present discussion we will not distinguish between these. We will assume that, in both instances, the final validation of this process is the person's better self-evaluation and commitment. As a result, he arrives at operational tactics that not only satisfy him but genuinely call forth from all aspects of himself, a cooperative engagement that brings about a successful resolution.

We can, then, look at the process by which the person attempts to know himself in a highly complex way as similar to that by which groups of friends working together would struggle to know their strengths and weaknesses. First of all, a person has to bring forward, either with the help of a counselor or through his own reflective ingenuity, as much information about himself, past and present, as he can possibly garner. We can apply personally the remark of Santayana that he who is ignorant

201

of history is destined to repeat it. A person cannot remain ignorant and unaware of what has happened to him in the past and the reasons, good or bad, why he had succeeded or failed. Otherwise he becomes a continued victim of his own self-ignorance. As he studies himself he begins to see that inappropriate reactions he made to various physiological, instinctive and emotional elements of himself often, in fact, misled and defeated him. He recognizes, too, that when he made judgments he was wisely guided by these same aspects of himself. Unless a person knows this about himself with subtlety and discrimination he is destined to be trapped in his own ignorance.

## THE PROCESS OF SELF-UNDERSTANDING

Continuing our consideration of the model of the relationship of friends to friends applied to the self, we can now draw upon the client-counselor relationship, especially as it aids us to trace the process of self-understanding. In the counselor-client relationship, the process begins with the client's reflecting upon various conflicting and confusing states. He gradually discovers binding, impeding, and often defeating emotional, instinctive, and physiological reactions. This leads, at a deeper penetration, to a recognition of what is good and positive in these reactions in place of what was simply self-defeating. The counselor's skill is a major factor in aiding the person to penetrate the initial conflict and confusion so he can identify and analyze the sources of these reactions. In the process the person is freed from the narrow binds which at first restricted him.

Eventually this self-survey and reflecting process leads to the uncovering of the fundamental self-investments— usually unconscious and so previously unrecognized—that are behind the emotional and instinctive conflicts. This happens because as these conflicts emerge, they can be seen more clearly and can be more adequately symbolized with the counselor's help. In every emotional, instinctive, and somatic reaction, the self has an investment or such a reaction would not occur. An uninvolved self would not have any reason to react at these inner personal levels. Only the involved self finds itself triggered off by such a situation.

What the counseling process does, among other things, is to disentangle this kind of self-investment both from the emotions that it produces and from a wide variety of involved personal circumstances. As a result, the client grows to recognize that behind the negative conflict, there is a significant, even if limited, value for him but in its present use, it is simply impeding or defeating him. If he reacts defensively, for example, at a primitive instinctive level, he realizes that he may be defending some element of insecurity but that, in fact, this kind of reaction defeats him in other broader aims. We saw a simple illustration of this earlier in the eye reflex demonstration where the person blinks and pulls his head back until he can trust leaving his eyes open because he realizes he is not going to be hit by the other person's hand.

The person taking counsel with himself will follow a similar process. That is, he will reflect on various elemental reactions and come to discriminate in these, the particular value or good for himself that they contain. At the same time he will recognize that they are often narrow and really inadequate, from a broader and more integrated view of himself. What the counselor does for the client then is to help him unravel the conflicts so that he can eventually make new self investments in whatever direction his best options lie.

## RELEASE THROUGH SYMBOLIZATION

When we define man, in the ancient sense, as a rational animal, we really mean that he is as well, a symbolic animal as we discussed in Chapter V. His rationality consists primarily in drawing upon singular and unique events and situations so as to broaden them out into more universal concepts and terms. In this more universal view of himself he also frees himself of the narrow binds in which the soma has him caught up so that he was unable to see beyond himself. His ability to reflect on himself is part and parcel of his capacity to symbolize his own situation. In proportion as he succeeds in an adequate verbal cognitive symbolization of what he sees happening to himself, he also succeeds in disentangling himself from the unique circumstances and events surrounding these happenings. In such proportion he is also free to investigate the basic good and values which this reaction contains.

Consequently, in man's own self-pursuit and survey, he will be able to reflect on himself in proportion as he can unhook himself from the particular situation he is in. He does this especially as he is able to symbolize his personal situation more universally, and so be freed from its narrow binds and constrictions. In the concept of man as a rational animal, then, the important realization is that man is also a symbolic animal. His ability to universalize enables him to free himself from his narrowness, to go onward and outward and to act on those aspects of himself which his verbal cognitive symbols more adequately reveal.

In order for a man to do this, it is essential that he trust each reaction in himself, no matter how immediately threatening or disturbing it may at first seem. He must trust that these reactions have some meaning and purpose.

204

As the client and the counselor, or friend and friend, trust one another, so a person begins a positive self-process by respecting each impulse and reaction in himself. This puts him in a position to initiate the symbolization process.

On the contrary, in proportion as he fails to trust each reaction in himself as having some value and significance, so he is kept in a self-defeating bind. Hostile as at first he may feel towards a reaction at the moment it occurs, by trusting that it still has some value, he will begin to take the steps which will gradually lead to a broader understanding of these narrowed reactions. He will, therefore, not only see their value but will be able to control and direct them to the more integrated, over-all good of his total self. This process of symbolization, of universalizing and of ultimately becoming free, then, is in proportion to man's ability to accept all of the reactions within himself, even the ones that might be at first self-defeating. In proportion as he is able to do this, he can ultimately arrive at integration with them. Until this symbolization process occurs, man is bound. When it occurs, as we can see from the counseling process, the person can begin to reflect upon his basic personal value system. He can then re-sort these values and consciously direct the self to over-all goals which an integrated self has accepted and approved.

The individual elements of the self, such as a particular somatic, physiological reaction or a particular defensive instinct, are only compulsive in proportion as the person is initially bound by the perception they imply. Reconsidering, as an example, the eye reflex illustration, the person's eyes blink and his head pulls back defensively only in proportion as he sees the object coming at his eye and therefore containing a threat to his eye. Simultaneously as his eye-blinking stops and his head does not pull back, he is also changing from a threat perception. He moves to a broader grasp that he is cooperating in an experiment and the experiment is not going to hurt his eye or embarrass him. He now sees it will in fact be a constructive, dignified experience. In proportion, then, as these perception interpretations occur, he relaxes, smiles and his eyes do not blink. There has been no change in the situation itself—the same action of waving one's hand in front of him continues, yet he is no longer defensive, threatened, or anxious.

Similarly, what seems to free the person with regard to primitive elements in himself is that he begins to trust their narrow value, even when they are constricting and victimizing him. Looking at them and respecting them, he is then consciously able to reflect upon and re-sort his whole self-investment. He can then consciously re-invest in broader purposes and aims. The narrow constricted focus gives way to a larger view. Even in complex personality conflicts, this same transition occurs through reflective symbolization. It is, therefore, the narrow constricting aspects of emotional, instinctive, or somatic reactions that turn out to be self-defeating, not the particular positive function which they, in fact, do perform.

As the process of symbolization goes on, the person sees himself more clearly in regard to his over-all personal good and so is more far-sighted about his goals. This in turn allows him to make new choices. It involves establishing values that better correspond to his real desires, and re-sorting previous values. He can, however, now make new personal investments as well, because he has a broader picture of himself and his situation from which to choose and better integration to accomplish his choices.

## SUPPRESSION

It is a common awareness, expressed in a variety of different ways, that another person can note things about oneself that it is difficult for the person himself to discover. This is highlighted in the phrase, "seeing ourselves as others see us." What the other person often can observe seems to fit recent psychological conceptions under the term "suppression." That is, the person can suppress things about himself and not consciously recognize them because they do not fit his own self-concept. These suppressed elements may be feelings or similar reactions at all basic levels of the self. But in fact these suppressed elements still show themselves in a type of conduct that is sometimes readily recognized by others. Yet the person himself is unaware of this. As a result of this suppressed state, he is often victimized by his inadvertance. What he is actually doing and how others are really reacting to him may be completely outside his conscious recognition. He cannot consciously accept these reactions since they are against a self-concept to which he is firmly committed.

One illustration of this, for example, is a common guilt-reaction that people can have at the death of an aged relative. Consciously they see themselves as deeply concerned about and caring for the person. In no way do they wish the person's death. Yet, in fact, the life situation has made the presence of the old person in the home quite burdensome, particularly as the illness progresses and no hope of recovery is possible. Consequently in reaction to the burden and difficulties of the old person's presence, a person can, in fact, be projecting relief at the elderly person's death. These wishes and desires—understandable as they may be—cannot be recognized consciously because they would go against the deep sense of respect

207

and regard that the person consciously holds towards the aged person. They may also seem to conflict with promises made earlier to take "good" care of the aged person.

Later on, however, after the expected death, these death-wish feelings, suppressed during all the time of the lingering illness, can now come forward but in the form of guilt and self-attack. So the person is deeply caught up and victimized by feeling profoundly guilty because he now recognizes that he did wish the person dead. He attacks himself now in the realization that it was a relief and perhaps a great relief when the person actually died.

Feelings then that in themselves are to be expected, such as those that the burden of an aged person would cause, can be suppressed as contrary to a conscious self-image. Yet these feelings and their expression could always have been apparent to others. Later they can come forward in distorted form and plague the person with intense guilt and self-rejection.

In seeking to understand and be a friend to himself then, a person can anticipate the same kind of complexities in suppressing elements that go against his self-image. Such suppressions will come up again in a self-attacking and self-defeating form. Rather than continuing to suppress reactions not in harmony with his self-image, he needs consciously to face himself and re-tailor a more congruent self-concept.

This kind of suppression of elemental impulses within the self is, of course, very different from control. Control is the conscious awareness that such impulses are there and that they go against one's self-image. Control is the result of a conscious process of taking counsel with the self and, as a result, such responses give way to the greater, overall purpose of the whole self. The popular expression of "swallowing one's anger," for example, suggests the idea of suppression. But controlling one's anger and using it constructively for a purpose and goal, would be the control of an emotional, instinctive, somatic state. But "swallowing" something is often suppression and so is likely to come back up in a disguised form. It can result in guilt, depression, self-humiliation, and in impediments to a person's goals and so is self-destructive and defeating. A person might do the same thing but in one instance it would be self-suppression and in the other, the result of conscious control. A person might, for example, not exhibit anger. But in one instance he "swallowed" it or suppressed it; in the other he simply chose to control it. The second instance would demonstrate an integrated self-determined action.

The biblical expression of a person being a "whited sepulchre" also seems to describe the concept of suppression. It conveys the notion of a rock sepulchre inside the self, that is, an intense self-encapsulation. It is smooth, extremely difficult to break open and contains the stench of death. Applying the analogy to suppression, the original distorted value has now become threatening and is suppressed. It is a corruptive force but is covered over in such a way that it cannot be seen or even reached easily—it is sealed off from immediate awareness. The self, however, still carrying this dead structure around with it, will be affected by it in subtle ways. In the biblical image, the suppressed material is all there and is represented by the body, bones and even suppressed stench. One might also see here that the biblical solution, "Let the dead bury the dead," is understood to mean the conscious recognition of this dead material and so removing it from its corruptive present effects.

## The Evaluative Process

The survey and inquiry into the self leads, as we have seen, to self-evaluation. In this process, a person on his own or with a counselor's skilled aid, not only reflects upon but judges and evaluates how he operates. As a result of this reflective symbolization of his life's situations, he sees a variety of individual goals and purposes. Some of these are in conflict with one another. Some he wills now to discard and some he still values and wishes to retain. Any individual struggling to know himself will go through stages of this kind of evaluation. One might use the analogy of a person going to a bank deposit box to investigate and study the present value of his investments, some of which he has inherited and some acquired earlier by himself. In this process he must also decide whether he wishes to keep some or all of these investments and those he cashes, he may wish to re-invest elsewhere.

Similarly, a person inherits cultural self-investments and values from his parents and family, the neighborhood, the school, his particular religious affiliation, and even the background of immigrant nationalities that his neighborhood or parental line represents. In addition, he has acquired earlier childhood self-investments which served a limited purpose and which he arrived at by trial and error. Many of these, however, may now be giving diminishing returns or may, in fact, be impeding the person. Until he has consciously understood this by a process of adequately symbolizing himself, he cannot do anything about it. This is the evaluative process that emerges out of reflective symbolization. The person's open trusting of his emotional, instinctive, and somatic reactions, impeding and threatening as they may appear at first, makes this evaluative reflection possible.

210

It is therefore not abstractly intellectualizing around goals and purposes that produces genuine self-evaluation, but in fact a person's penetration and understanding of himself at emotional, instinctive, and somatic levels. Basic defense reactions, for example, or primitive sexual drives, resentments, and envies of others, hostilities and resistances coming even from early childhood, these can actually be the real determinants of where the self is invested. If these are not uncovered, then by merely intellectualizing around what he wants and what his goals are, he is simply "rationalizing" and so getting further away from real self re-cognition.

## THE INTELLECTUALIZED VS. THE OPERANT IDEAL

As a person recognizes his present basic values he is free to redirect the self to them whereas he may previously simply have intellectualized about himself. He was still, however, victimized by his unconscious, because unrecognized, earlier operant system. What determines where one will make his new and present self-investment is the process of re-cognizing (in the hyphenated sense of "cognizing again") his real self. This is the basis for determining where his future self-investment will be. By adequately "cognizing" this, he is assuring himself of a better and more genuine self-fulfillment. An abstractive type of intellectualizing about the self is drawn, not from a realistic engagement with the self, but from ideals borrowed from outside the self. This will, at best, offer potential goals for the self to consider. At worse it can be a source of guilt and attack against the actual operational self. In any case, it will not, in itself, aid the person to any re-sorting and re-evaluation of the basic operational systems that are actually guiding his life.

On the contrary this kind of intellectualization can also

211

lead to suppression, since it can be responsible for a false self-ideal. This can result in a self-concept that fails to admit and so open itself up to the real operant elements that actually determine the way the self is acting. This would be the source of a rationalization process which justifies a personal status quo. Such a self-concept and intellectualized ideal blocks out by refusing to look at what may be obvious, especially to others. The kind of a bind in which one intellectualizes around an idealized operational system, but in fact is governed by a much more primitive negatively toned system, can be a source of initial conflict. The evaluation process will bring out the previously repressed but actual operating system. The intellectualizing self keeps the self from its real operational-self and so is responsible for a split in the person which often causes guilt.

We have already referred to the manner in which the counselor "re-cognizes" the emotions or instincts or primitive somatic elements that the person has described verbally. We can apply this to the way a person becomes a knowing, understanding friend to himself. This "cognizing" of the self is the conscious recognition of the real operant systems in the self as against the prior intellectualizing process that gave a false self-concept. This kind of self-justification and rationalization preserved the false self-ideal or self-concept from any genuine awareness of the self. It is a "cognizing" with respect, trust, and self-regard in contrast to the fear, hostility, and suppression of the prior intellectualizing rationalization system. It is in "cognizing" each element of the personality and respecting it as having some particularized good that the "cognizing" process grows to appreciate each element of the self.

This results in an adequate, reflective symbolization on

212

the real "flecting" and "tracting" self. In place of the narrow bind and particular emotional situation, broader operational systems and goals are developed that are more truly adequate and fulfilling for the whole integrated self. It is in the "cognizing" process that the real operational self is given recognition.

What emerges in the counseling process is a new client self-commitment. Such self-commitment can result too, in a person's becoming a friend to himself. Previously, in the suppressed state the self is often really committed more to defensive emotional or somatic responses which actually direct and control the whole self. The person, however, consciously does not admit this. Instead, he intellectualizes a non-defensive self idea which, desirable as it is, he has not in fact incorporated in himself. Such a person lacks an incarnational process. The ideal remains non-incarnational and never comes to his own flesh-and-blood operational system. In not admitting this to himself, the person rationalizes and so deceives himself that these ideas are, in fact, operant and incarnational in himself.

This resistance is also resistance to admitting his real incarnate self. Yet one is unable to understand why he is not achieving the ideals that he has been holding up for himself and why, in a final state, he is guilty, hostile, and frustrated towards himself. As long as he intellectualizes and rationalizes about what he should be doing he can blame other elemental aspects of himself for having betrayed him and failed to aid him effectively to fulfill this self-ideal.

## THE TACTIC PERIOD

In contrast to this, the "cognizing" process comes to grips first with what the self is truly invested in. It does not matter how elemental or primitive the source of that

213

investment may be. Nor does it matter if these sources are in childhood or in an inherited culture. Such realistic "cognizing," discovers where, in fact, the self is really invested. And once that is discovered, then it is possible to reflect on this actual "flecting" and abstract from this actual "tracting" and so arrive at a broader awareness of the real operant self.

As a result of what we are calling the "cognizing" process, the self can then proceed to a "tactic" phase, to use Aristotle's term. This concerns new plans and actions devised around the person's immediate life circumstances. In contrast to ineffective intellectualized ideals, the "cognizing" process results in operational tactics which are genuinely aimed at the person's real goals and purposes. But this is now an incarnate investment with real appreciation and knowledgeable trust of all aspects of his whole unique self. This positive self-attitude towards the real operant self frees the self from the need to be bitter and hostile towards those elements of the self that previously seemed self-defeating. This is an incarnational acceptance of the self by the ego, in contrast to the previous rejection of the self in a commitment to an abstract self-ideal. It is also a redemptive entering into and accepting all aspects of the operant self. This is because the incarnational process recognizes real worth and meaning in every fundamental element that the self has. Many of these elemental responses in the self have narrow particular goods. The "cognizing" system appreciates the primitive original value of these reactions; at the same time, it can recognize when previous operational systems have reached points of diminishing returns, or of no returns at all. This results in reinvesting the self in a new kind of tactic or operational system geared, in an incarnational redemptive sense, to all elements of himself. This especially includes those whom

214

he had previously suppressed and would not recognize.

An incarnational acceptance of the self no longer says, "I am disgusted with myself." It is no longer negative and divided. It no longer shows resistance to becoming incarnate. The self, then, is more open and so more able to make a choice in terms of reinvestment. It can determine more effectively what it's new operational system will be. Previously, it was too caught up in its own negative non-incarnational self to make any such positive investment. Friendship with the self then, demands a genuine trust in, respect, and regard for every element of the personality, even the most primitive. All these elements work towards the good of the self, when the person is a true friend to himself. This is very different from a primitive fear-anxiety-threat feeling. In this anxiety state mysterious aspects of the self are always seen as inimical and threatening and so must always be guarded. Here we have the symbols of wild animals or the notion of keeping prisoners under control, or some similar model.

Obviously the model of friendship changes this and produces trust and security towards all aspects of the self, as among friends working together. One does not demand of the friend more than he is capable of doing, thereby causing him to defeat himself; rather, one respects him in those things which he truly can do, and one trusts him in this. One is careful not to expect more or less than this.

## THE PROPHETIC EGO

In friendship to the self, the individual elements of the self, particularly the emotions, tend in varying degrees to be microscopic in their awareness of what is good for the self. By contrast, the cognitive ego is more macroscopic in grasping the overall good and direction of the self. A final resolution strives to combine all these elements of the self

215

so they interrelate, balance one another, and harmonize.

These elements of the self, however, do not constitute a stable field. The self is undergoing constant change in both itself and in the atmospheric environment in which it is operating. Hence the self is in a changing operational field. When what we might call a "prophetic" aspect of self-awareness begins to sense change in the direction of a new process, the over-all self begins to be uncomfortable with the status quo. This can also include—if not suppressed—discomfort with operational systems that may have worked well up until that point. This, in fact, might even be a kind of constructive guilt and self-attack as well as a constructive discomfort—particularly as failure, frustration and defeat begin as a result of present inadequate operational plans.

Aquinas, talking about treasuring and husbanding the doubt, catches the value of the prophetic ego in its discomfort with the way things are. Such self-doubt and discomfort can lead to an end point where a whole new operational plan may be necessary.

This type of prophetic ego could then also be considered the initiating ego. It makes the self uncomfortable with a system that until now, may have operated well. It may even continue to operate well as long as the basic factors through self-doubt and discomfort remain the same. At the same time, the prophetic initiating self is preparing the way for a new adaptation of the self and a new tactic or operational plan.

The prophetic initiating self therefore can be disturbing and threatening in its first reactions. This initial inimical tone must be removed so this phase of the self is regarded by the operating self as a friendly, respectful guide. What has been established and secure for the self is now undergoing change. The operant self, overcoming its

216

threat and anxiety in face of possible change, opens itself up to the basic wisdom of this prophetic and anticipatory aspect of the self. In so opening itself it begins to acquire a macroscopic view. This is necessary not only to clarify what the prophetic ego senses, but also to make preparations for change. A more adequate type of operational system must be devised to correspond to a new operational field.

## THE SELF AS COMMUNITY

The self is not to be conceived of as an isolated ego against primitive wild forces that must be kept under control, nor as a guard in a prison subduing prisoners, nor even as a kind of politician who, by various forms of strategy, placates and quiets quasi-rebellious citizens. Rather friendship with the self imitates the way a well-governed community secures the maximum cooperation of all by persuading each citizen that the agreed views and judgments of the community are the best means by which they can relate to one another and to themselves.

We could define the ideal view goal of the self then, as a positive, incarnate, redemptive convalidating community. By these terms we would mean that, in the light of a true friend to a friend, there are no elements in the self that are really unfriendly or inimical to the self. Even though various aspects of the self may be viewed as microscopic in their primitive elemental awareness, or prophetic in the unrest they create as they sense change emerging, or ego-cognitive in their macroscopic view, they can all be coordinated towards the over-all good of the person. They can all work together like a genuine community of friends, each convalidating positively the worth and meaning of the other. The person himself, however, in his totality, must take into consideration the fact that any one phase of self-awareness alone can be limited and inadequate. Each must be modified and coordinated with other aspects of the ego.

In addition this process involves a healing self-incarnation. The cognitive ego tends, in the first inimical reaction, to keep itself removed from, because it sees as threatening, the incarnate elements of the self. Later, however, it positively invokes all these elements of the self, openly trusting them and respectfully regarding them. This is the incarnational healing process.

The effect of this is a sense of the worth of all aspects of the self. No element of the self can respond negatively as if it could feel rejected by, or suspected by, other aspects of the self. The "I" can then move from voicing—in our example—"I am disgusted with myself," or "I am afraid of myself," to "I am pleased," and "I am secure with myself." The "I" or the cognitive self has entered into an incarnate redemptive positive convalidation of all parts of the self.

We can think of man then not only as a social animal, in Aristotle's way of viewing him, but even more as a community-self. Perhaps part of what may mislead us in our approach to ourselves and thus may make the elements of the self appear so threatening, is that we insist on seeing ourselves according to the model of an isolated individual. It is as if we saw ourselves only one way and as having only one view and reaction—as if we were "monoscopal." But, in fact, we are not monoscoped, but highly complicated, "community-scoped." These various interwoven "scopes" are necessary to an adequate view. For appropriate response, they must be harmonized and interrelated before any self-coordination is possible.

Our initial misconstruction of ourselves as simple and monoscopic causes us to misconstrue much of what happens to us. Rather we need to view ourselves as a complex community in which the conscious, cognitive ego is, at best, a macroscopic element. But a variety of microscopic elements must be appreciated, trusted, and accepted before any harmonized fulfillment of a community-self is possible. The cognitive ego, rather than seeing itself as the only positive element surrounded by primitive elements that are inimical, must listen to all of the elements of the self. It must strive redemptively to give worth, respect, and understanding to what each represents, granting that each, at its own level, may be operating from a microscopic view of the whole situation.

## THE "EPISCOPIC" SELF

We can also add here the notion of "episcopic," as conveying something distinct from "macroscopic." One might raise the question as to why one needs the term "episcopic" in this discussion of the self. What does "episcopic" add to what we are saying? It seems to suggest a new epistemological element in the operational aspects of the self related both to itself and to others. To use the analogy of constructing a building, it is the contractor who is the "episcopic" person in that he is the central operationally oriented person. Like the director of a symphony, he pulls together all the parts of the building and sees that it gets built as a whole. He is not simply concerned about particular activities, like the carpenter or the electrician, who only see the building in terms of the things which they themselves do.

If we contrast the contractor of a building with the architect, we have a further notion of "episcope" rather than simply macroscope. The contractor, as the operationally overseeing person, would have the same kind of integrated view as that of the architect. He would see the details of the building, as they fit together. But this is not a view that will lend itself directly to operation. In this the contractor has a different type of over-all view from that of the architect.

The same might be said of the "episcopic" self. The "episcope" deals operationally with the mass convergence of all the individual elements, but in a way that makes them a unity, rather than breaking them up into particularized parts. The espicopic view is the view that takes the mass and operates with it effectively.

When the total person operates adequately, he brings activity to successful fruition; final operational decisions succeed because they express the composite will of the harmonized, unified self-complexity or self-community. Such a person is workman, craftsman, architect and contractor to himself. He is not merely an intellectual in the idealistic-abstractionist sense. He does not simply hold to and operate on an over-all macroscopic view coming purely from abstraction and reflection. Therefore he need not necessarily be intellectually bright, in the usual sense of such a term. Rather he has acquired a skilled feel of the right moment at which to make personally adequate decisions. An intellectualized self-view, then, would be misleading. This is the kind of view of the self which comes simply from reflecting and abstracting without adequate "flecting" and "tracting" in real experience with all elements of the self. The way in which the self coordinates and harmonizes all its elements in an adequate tactic or operational system is a function of the rational cognitive self but in a rationality which is geared to reaching and integrating the whole operational self. In fact, unless this is clearly understood, overmuch intellectualizing can actually paralyze the self and impede it from any real operation. Such a self endlessly meditating about itself is trying "to come to grips" with itself, in the

220

popular term. But in fact it never actually "grips" the self and so puts the self into action. The cognitive, operational directive of the self comes at the right moment of intuition. It plunges the self into operation, feeling as well as knowing a harmony that has emerged from integrated thinking about the self.

## SUMMARY

One is friend to himself then by "cognizing" respectfully all the positive factors that every aspect and element of himself actually contains. In seeing oneself inimically so that one is hostile, angry, or disgusted with oneself, a person attributes his failures to and so sees as negative, various basic elements of the self, somatic, instinctive, or emotional. After genuine "cognizing" of himself, he grows to re-cognize that the self-defeating factors have been his own conscious doings. In rebelling against his "myself" in such terms as "I am disgusted with myself," a person fails to appreciate and understand the "myself" in a way that would result in a truly invested operational system. His ego, the "I" that is disgusted, is ineffectively protesting against a rationalized self-regarding process. This is anti-incarnational and so fundamentally rejecting of many basic self elements.

In becoming a friend to oneself one openly trusts the elements of the "myself." These are, in fact, also indicative of one's self-commitment. Once a person has consciously grasped this, he can, if he so chooses, begin to withdraw the investment of the self and change his operational system and life tactics. At the same time, he must arrive at a truly incarnational, redemptive regard for himself. This would be the description of being a true friend to himself. From this follows the basic dynamic and potential of loving others and God.

# INDEX